W9-BIY-196

The Asian Miracle, Myth, and Mirage

The Asian Miracle, Myth, and Mirage

THE ECONOMIC SLOWDOWN IS HERE TO STAY

Bernard Arogyaswamy

QUORUM BOOKS
Westport, Connecticut • London

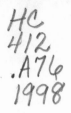

Library of Congress Cataloging-in-Publication Data

Arogyaswamy, Bernard.
   The Asian miracle, myth, and mirage : the economic slowdown is here to
stay / Bernard Arogyaswamy.
      p.   cm.
   Includes bibliographical references and index.
   ISBN 1–56720–127–X (alk. paper)
   1. Asia—Economic conditions—1945–   2. Economic forecasting—
Asia.   I. Title.
HC412.A724   1998
338.95—dc21   97–41002

British Library Cataloguing in Publication Data is available.

Library of Congress Catalog Card Number: 97–41002
ISBN: 1–56720–127–X

First published in 1998

Quorum Books, 88 Post Road West, Westport, CT 06881
An imprint of Greenwood Publishing Group, Inc.

Printed in the United States of America

The paper used in this book complies with the
Permanent Paper Standard issued by the National
Information Standards Organization (Z39.48–1984).

10 9 8 7 6 5 4 3 2 1

To the memory of Mariadas Ruthnaswamy,
educator, thinker, statesman . . . and wise grandfather.

Contents

Preface

When President Clinton traveled to the APEC (Asia Pacific Economic Co-operation) meeting at Manila in November 1997, it reinforced both his administration's resolve to commingle trade with diplomacy and the importance of the Asia Pacific Region to American economic interests. After all, the United States trades more across the Pacific than it does across the Atlantic. No reminder is needed, of course, that Asia is where the action is and has been for a while. Unless one has been as sequestered as a jury member in a high-profile criminal trial, one cannot help being submerged under a torrent of information and opinion lauding Asian achievements and rejoicing over its even more brilliant future. Amid all the hoopla generated by corporate and political leaders, a few voices of skepticism have been raised, though rarely heeded.

Having heard some of these dissenting voices, I decided to take a closer look at how Asian nations got to where they are and whether they have the wherewithal to keep doing more of the same in the years to come. This book is the outcome of that search.

What I discovered is that a cocktail of Eastern arrogance and Western admiration, laced with generous doses of greed on both sides, can be a heady brew. It can blind us to what we do not wish to see. The gentle and protective hand of the government nurtured businesses in one Asian country after another and continues to ride to the rescue of its local champions whenever needed. That was perfectly fine when Asia was a well-kept secret, when the communist threat mesmerized the West and when the gap to be bridged was large. As "catch-up" has progressed, the need to develop new technologies independently and to conduct innovative research becomes critical if a nation is not to be frozen in a state of permanent "catch-up."

In this as well as in managing organizations that can undertake the cutting-edge research that will enable them to compete worldwide, Asian countries have a long way to go. The nation-state is not moribund, and governments are often hyperactive, but they can take their countries only so far. To top it all, Asian societies have feet planted in different centuries and have yet to solve—or, in some cases, even face—the moral, social and cultural problems of rapid growth. If you throw in the possibility of democratization in hitherto authoritarian nations and of provincialism in the larger ones (e.g., China and India), the future of Asia begins to look very uncertain indeed.

Incidentally, the book was conceived, and much of the manuscript completed, before financial convulsions hit Thailand, Malaysia, Indonesia and other neighboring nations. At any rate, as this work points out, there are more serious maladies afflicting Asian nations than financial speculation gone awry or irresponsible lending by banks. Worrying about Asia's present problems is analogous to the captain of the *Titanic* being upset that choppy seas might ruin the shipboard festivities planned during the voyage. There is worse to come. Much worse.

My intent is not to be critical or harsh about Asia past, present or future. I do intend, however, to warn that much needs to be done and needs to be changed to ensure a bright future. Western countries ought to be aware that nationalism thrives on Asian soil. American and European firms will be entertained there only so long as they have something to offer. Once foreign multinationals have outlived their usefulness, they will be politely shown the door, World Trade Organization (WTO) or no WTO.

The notion of writing this book first crossed my mind while I was teaching my course on the United States and Asia at Le Moyne College. I am indebted to my students over the years in this course and all the other courses like Strategic Management, and Total Quality Management that I have taught at this institution. I am grateful to John Doutt for his encouragement and suggestions and to Elizabeth Lukacs of the Le Moyne College library for sending material my way whenever she ran across anything relevant. Sharyn Knight did the manuscript in double-quick time, often working at home to speed things up. I thank her for her attention to detail and willingness to process my often chaotic manuscript.

1

Miracle?

SUCCESS IS INFECTIOUS

Judging from the numerous books and the spate of television programs dedicated to the wondrous rise of Asia and the excitement generated among the ranks of corporate leaders in the West at the thought of millions of new, grasping consumers, one could say that Asia has, in a sense, come of age economically. Few will dispute the extraordinary growth achieved by most Asian countries over the past quarter century. Even those nations that missed the bus earlier—India and the Philippines come to mind—are making sure they hop on before it's too late. The evidence of success is too obvious to deny or ignore. A chorus of praise has naturally, perhaps justifiably, been heaped on the Asian work ethic, its peoples' prudence and patience, governmental wisdom and virtue and, in general, apparently extraordinary abilities, traits and policies that bid fair to leave the West far behind. A few voices of dissent have also been heard: Paul Krugman, an economist of no mean repute, has argued, for instance, that Asia's explosive growth has been fueled primarily by an increase in inputs—labor, education, capital generated through savings—and not by increases in productivity.[1] Krugman and others who share his opinion assert that success resting on this sort of foundation cannot last.[2] Certainly, a pinch of skepticism is healthy, but is this an overdose of it? Perhaps—but the optimistic rush to judgement that seems to characterize most assessments of Asian nations' future needs to be tempered with caution and an understanding of how they got where they are.

But I am getting ahead of myself. We should properly begin our exploration of Asia's magnificent achievements by describing them in all their glory. We will then try to understand how they all came about. Our final quest will be to determine if Asia's present presages an even brighter future. Will its momentum endure long enough for Asian nations to aspire to world leadership and to displace the United States from that position?

To begin with, most generalizations about a continent as diverse as Asia must be taken with generous doses of salt. Dissimilarities within Asia are at least as numerous and striking as are commonalities. Singapore and Hong Kong, for instance, bear a greater resemblance in terms of living standards to Tokyo and, indeed, to London and Chicago than they do to Beijing or Bombay. The Asian racial mix enfolds within it the Han Chinese, the Malay, the Semite and the Caucasian. Diverse religious allegiances co-exist, sometimes not so peacefully, across the face of Asia, some parts being fervent, even fanatical, in their beliefs, while others are prosaic in their attitude to faith, viewing it as little more than another mundane piece of their workaday lives. Politically, too, Asian nations are spread all over the spectrum, stretching from authoritarian to democratic, from repressive to permissive. Despite the marked and obvious differences within the conti-nent—differences that are, literally, continental—a few common features are distinguishable as well.

One pattern that has clearly emerged in some countries and is discernible among most of the rest is the recognition that economic growth solves (or moderates) a host of problems. The days are long gone when Asian leaders like Sukarno or Nehru used to lecture the rest of the world on morality, economics, nuclear weapons and anything else they felt moved to weigh in on. Most are too concerned with internal problems of poverty, divisiveness and political stability to take more than a superficial interest in interna-tional intangibles. Of course, countries like Japan, Taiwan, Singapore, Hong Kong and South Korea can afford to criticize whomever they please, but each of these countries has frictions with, or concerns about, its neigh-bor(s), making it wary of antagonizing potential allies. Even Malaysia's ebullient prime minister Mahathir Mohammed, who is quick to tell the West, in particular the United States, not to interfere in Asian countries' internal affairs—civil rights are the most frequent bone of contention—is careful to recognize on which side his military bread is buttered. The rise of a powerful China, the possibility of Japan's rearming, Russian instabil-ity, uncertainty in Korea and the resultant dependence on American naval power and airpower[3] have undoubtedly helped focus the mind on what's economically possible, leaving ideological posturing to the dwindling ranks of the world's autarkies. It has become clearer than ever before that dip-lomatic and military power flows from a soaring economy. By most indi-cators, that's exactly what most countries in Asia are proud possessors of—or are poised to lay claim to.

It is common knowledge that many Asian countries have experienced remarkable economic growth over the past quarter century. Japan and

South Korea are obvious cases in point. The former is a member of the "First World," a world in which people, by and large, live in comfort, if not relative luxury. South Korea, while not quite in the same league, is clearly not a less developed country (LDC) either.[4] Its standard of living, its ability to design and make a range of products using cutting-edge technology (even if few have been developed indigenously—but more of that later), the desire and the ability shown by the Korean conglomerates (*chaebol*) to invest in, and market, their products abroad, even in Europe and North America, all combine to set South Korea apart from all its Asian neighbors save Japan. These two nations, in fact, are in a class of their own, and not even the newly industrialized countries (NICs) of Taiwan, Hong Kong and Singapore can yet aspire to join their exclusive club, even if their per capita incomes are higher. While the NICs or Asian tigers—call them what you will—have achieved remarkable rates of gross domestic product (GDP) growth and stunning improvements in living standards, they do not seem to have the ability to mount a challenge to foreign multinational corporations (MNCs) abroad. They are likely to remain economic powers for the foreseeable future, but only in their own backyards, Taiwan's investments in countries like Thailand notwithstanding. A notch lower in the pecking order of prosperity and power are the South Korea wannabes—Malaysia, Indonesia, Thailand, with Philippines and perhaps Vietnam looking in on the party, hoping to be invited in. Malaysia, Indonesia and Thailand are no laggards in economic growth, though per capita incomes in these countries trail those in Hong Kong and Singapore, partly due to their larger and ethnically more diverse and divided populations. The two city-nations, moreover, built their fortunes, initially, as entrepôt ports, facilitating trade between East and West, with Hong Kong's making a killing on southern China's debut as a player on the world's economic stage. Malaysia, Indonesia and Thailand are, indeed, prosperous and prominent members, along with Singapore, of the increasingly vocal Association of Southeast Asian Nations (ASEAN), a group of eight faced with the unenviable task of framing policies and procedures to benefit all while upsetting no one. The trio's rise was due, in no small part (like their East Asia mentors before them), to government policies and actions to stimulate exports, restrict imports and enhance indigenous technological capabilities. However, unlike the Japanese, Koreans and Taiwanese, the Southeast Asian ascent has, particularly of late, been driven by the influx of foreign capital from both Asian and Western[5] sources.

The Philippines, which has dallied with both autocratic and democratic rule and has had an enduring relationship with the United States, has jumped on the bandwagon of Asian capitalism but recently. It seems to be following in the footsteps of some of its successful neighbors by establishing special zones for development, by tempting foreign capital and ideas to make a home there and by projecting a general pro-business, open-for-business attitude.[6] The United States is beginning to recover from its Vietnamese hangover, and the government there, communist at least in name, has been actively cultivating MNCs regardless of national origin. However, although the pundits often declare that foreign investment is *not* a zero-sum game and that firms should invest wherever high returns are likely, the reality is that most firms face resource constraints, acquire competence in particular markets and are often reluctant to deal with risks inherent to new market entries. Vietnam must now, therefore, compete with neighboring and distant countries, both successful and aspiring to success, for attention.

No such predicament confronts China. After nearly three decades of seclusion, stagnation and schizophrenia, China's first halting steps toward free enterprise, taken in 1978, have turned into a full gallop.[7] Foreign investment does not have to be solicited. Investment proposals, so to speak, come knocking, almost pleading to be allowed in. General Motors, Procter & Gamble, IBM, Honda and Toyota are among the corporate heavyweights that have a big stake in the Chinese market. The bulk of the foreign investment thus far, however, has come from Hong Kong, which has also served as the conduit through which skilled labor, technology and managerial capabilities have crossed over to the mainland. The investments made in the special economic zones (SEZs), particularly in Guangdong, by the expatriate Chinese based in Hong Kong (and, to a lesser extent, by the Taiwanese) provided the seed money and business foundation on which China's growth in the last decade or so has been based. The belief in individual enterprise and the desire for wealth formed a happy amalgam in post-Mao China. Exports have shown meteoric rates of increase, and China's trade surplus with the United States has come to rival Japan's. Per capita GDP has doubled over a period of seven years, though the rate of increase varies geographically. Rising living standards have created a lucrative domestic market, from which foreign companies—Procter & Gamble is a prominent example—have been quick to profit. A crystal gazer might detect a few potential trouble spots in China's future. Among the clouds on the horizon are the state-owned enterprises, which continue to kick and scream at the prospect of their baptism in capitalistic beliefs and practices, the uncertainty over leadership succession and political structure, the increasing recalcitrance of the provinces and their reluctance to kowtow to the center and the widening regional economic disparity that has resulted in considerable migration and discontent. But these areas of concern should in no way detract from the glowing testament to wise policy making and free economic action that modern China offers. Rather, the transformation in China is all the more remarkable for having occurred *in spite of* these constraints and deterrents. (Though the desire for provincial autonomy has, in part, followed from rising incomes and tax revenues, centripetal tendencies have also been curtailed somewhat by the fear, so to speak, of killing the goose that laid the golden egg.) Even more amazing is the fact that the unbridled growth of the past decade or so followed not long after the last convulsions of the cultural revolution. Some might argue that the country was ready for order and stability, which was no doubt true, but, all the same, it needed farseeing leadership to enact a set of economic reforms that energized the population and carefully repaired the tattered fabric of society.[8]

No one can question the success of China's reforms in galvanizing the economy. The jury is still out on India.[9] The policy changes initiated in 1991, when the country was on the verge of defaulting on interest payments on its foreign debt, have not quite played themselves out as yet. Numerous industries have been opened up to foreign investment as well as majority ownership, the regimen of quotas in production has been dismantled, public sector (government-owned) firms are downsizing and/or equity in them is being sold to the public, stock ownership is soaring, and large, privately-owned Indian companies are girding themselves to do battle with MNCs. The growth rate of the economy has, however, come nowhere near the double-digit mark attained—and sustained—by many Asian economies (e.g., South Korea, China, Malaysia and Thailand) over the past two decades. For most of the 1980s and halfway into the 1990s, India's high-water mark for GDP growth has been 7%, but there are signs that the "Hindu rate of growth" is becoming a thing of the past.[10] The projection for the second half of this last decade of the century is that increases in GDP will be close to the 10% rate that signifies the coming-of-age of a developing economy. Exports, moreover, are beginning to demonstrate diversity and robustness, both causes for optimism that the defensiveness of "import substitution" has given way to the venturesomeness of seeking and welcoming dependence on foreign customers. The autarkic mentality dies hard, though. Exporting goods and services, whether they consist of textiles, machines or software, is undoubtedly an attractive prospect. But, policymakers and politicians are often reluctant to allow imports of capital equipment and raw materials to create the ability to generate exports. Even when the battle to allow imports—which may initially exceed exports—has been won, the will and the ability to improve the water and electricity availability, all forms of transportation and the rest of the infrastructure may be weak or even lacking. India is experiencing such a debate, made more intense and messy by the country's democratic system. The technological and investment gap, however, makes infrastructural investment and imports unavoidable if foreign and domestic demand is to be continuously satisfied. Privatization of power generation, telecommunications and even roads, under a BOT (build, operate, transfer) regimen, helps induce MNCs to invest large sums of money—in India as elsewhere—drawn by returns on the order of 15% over the long term. With the savings rate rising above the 30% mark, stock ownership becoming a passion with millions of urban

Indians and banks seeking prospective borrowers for industrial loans, the pool of funds available for investment is getting deeper and wider. India is about 15 years behind China in market reform years, though it does have many of the accoutrements of a democratic free enterprise society that are essential to consolidate the reform regime—small and large businesses, a judicial system, a responsible electorate, as well as skilled labor and managerial capabilities.

Asians of all hues are justifiably proud of what has been accomplished on their continent, particularly, at least until now, in its eastern portion. The elevation in standards of living, improvements in health care and longevity, educational achievements, the amelioration of poverty and so on have severed the vicious circle of hardship that was deemed inevitable by and for the many. Coupled with what is widely perceived by Asian politicians, if not their constituents, as the moral decay of the West, invidious comparisons are often drawn. Endemic drug use, pervasive crime and alarmingly high divorce rates are among the numerous symptoms cited of a declining Western civilization. Righteous Asian anger at the West often bubbles up in response to economic and political criticism of the nouveau riche Orient. The Japanese, against whom numerous complaints have been filed and a variety of penalties threatened unless their markets are made less difficult to enter, often respond by pointing out deficiencies in the American way of life.[11] Shareholders who demand immediate returns, dating in secondary schools, a lack of corporate loyalty and even keeping automated teller machines open at night have come under fire from Japanese hard-liners irked by criticism of their nation and its policies. Among the recent arrivals at the Asian tea party (only the wealthy and almost-wealthy can attend), the primary bone of contention has generally been about their political systems. China, Singapore, Indonesia, Thailand and even Malaysia have, to varying degrees, come under fire from Western critics for human rights violations. (Taiwan and South Korea, both democracies, have recently had their names expunged from this dishonor roll.) Nations that have felt the sting of foreign disapproval typically retort that their critics should stop interfering in others' internal affairs, respect the sovereignty of an independent nation and realize that norms developed in America or Europe are not transferable to Asian locales. Some might argue that countries run by authoritarian regimes seem to become defensive about their treatment of their own people. Not only are countries like China, Indonesia and Singapore clear about where they are headed, but they are equally clear that their social and economic role models will not be America, Holland or Britain. Resentment against Western countries often assumes racial overtones, implying—or even explicitly asserting—that the powers whose day has passed may be showing their unhappiness and anxiety over having to make way for the emerging nations, to which the future, presumably, belongs. Are the advanced nations of today on the fast track to becoming has-beens? Can Asia continue to rise at its present historic rates? Will Asian countries succeed only by rejecting Western example and experience?

These and similar questions are considered and addressed later in this book, but at this point it would be instructive and useful to assess how some of the high-performing nations (and their optimistic imitators) in Asia have gotten where they are.

THE SINCEREST FORM OF FLATTERY

The end of the cold war was greeted with a collective sigh of relief and the reinforcement of the conviction that democracy and free enterprise had triumphed over authoritarian rule and planned economies. The assertion made during the 1992 presidential campaign that Japan had won the cold war seemed little more than an epigram. Japan, though undoubtedly an economic powerhouse, was no superpower in terms of military clout or political influence. Why, even in Asia, their own backyard, the Japanese were widely feared and hated. How could the ideology-less Japanese have won a war in which they were not even combatants? While such skepticism over the influence the Japanese have exercised over their Asian neighbors is far from uncommon, a cursory glance at the genesis of their growing muscle should be persuasive evidence to the contrary.

The efficient and inscrutable Japanese, pragmatic and aspiritual though they appear, did espouse a belief system we like to call capitalism. Whether you call it Confucian or Japanese capitalism makes little difference. It can be distinguished from the Western, particularly American, form of capitalism in one significant feature. The government is central to the stellar performance of Japanese capitalism.[12] If the Japanese economy were a movie, the government would be the director. Both the broad themes and message, as well as the selection of actors and how they play their roles, are in the hands of the directorial government. That is, the politicians and bureaucrats in charge designed macroeconomic measures (which had an impact across the board) and crafted industrial policy (whose focus was industry-specific) in order to achieve *national goals*. The insular, homogeneous Japanese circled their wagons, so to speak, in the aftermath of the Second World War and the Occupation. The *kohutai*, or national will, which, prior to the war, had—in an apparent display of mass hysteria, as some describe it—imbued the country with a militant, arrogant spirit, now coalesced around a mission of catch-up. Not only the government but companies, too, articulated this intent clearly and often. Toyota, for instance, set a goal of catching up with Ford by the end of the 1970s. Komatsu wanted to "encircle Cat," and Xerox was targeted by a slew of copying copier-makers.

Despite the antipathy many Koreans feel for Japan, Korea was quick to adopt similar national goals and an almost identical role for the government in achieving it. Predominantly agrarian societies, Japan, Korea and Taiwan undertook varying degrees of land reform to forestall possible disgruntlement among farmers. The exhortations to unite (against North Korea or China, to catch up with the West, recover lost national honor, etc.) and the shortage of consumer goods, let alone luxuries, meant that surpluses were saved. In Korea, the government helped the creation of suitable firms and facilitated their success through preferential contracts, tax breaks, subsidies and so on. In Japan, the corporations that were to epitomize Japan in later years—Toyota, Mitsubishi, Matsushita—already existed or were formed by entrepreneurs (e.g., Honda). The expatriate Chinese brought their business acumen and family connections to bear in the mushrooming of relatively small firms on Taiwan's road to fame and fortune. Malaysia, Indonesia, Thailand and China have subscribed and submitted, in ways designed to suit their specific needs, to government-directed capitalism.

The "Asian miracle,"[13] as the World Bank has termed it, therefore, has all too earthly, even socialist, origins. Born of the desire to be the equal of the West and orchestrated by a force that created and molded markets, provided advice and made suggestions and even made know-how and capital available where necessary, the phenomenon had much that was remarkable, though little supernatural about it. Mundane actions like the establishment of special economic zones, the encouragement of exports (by providing tax breaks and subsidies to exporters), the curtailment of imports (except for exporters), stimulation of domestic investment through savings and so on require forethought, determination and patience. The incentive to work hard may be intrinsic to the labor force (as in the case of Japan) or be alloyed with extrinsic motivation, as was true to differing degrees in the instances of China, Korea, Taiwan and the other countries of East and Southeast Asia. A question that arises is, Why did this part of the world start industrializing and developing rapidly rather than, say, countries in Africa? Is there something peculiarly Asian in the phenomenon, something that will sustain its dramatic economic expansion into the future?

If all that it took for some East and Southeast Asian nations to create soaring economies was for their governments to design and direct their growth, motivating their populations through intrinsic and/or extrinsic means, why was the phenomenon confined almost exclusively to Asia? Was this the only part of the world where sensible governments and disciplined, diligent people were to be found? The response to the first part of the latter question is a qualified yes if one compares them to governments in Africa and Latin America, which either adopted doctrinaire socialism and killed their citizens' initiative or became radically corporativistic and plutocratic. Human rights and free market principles were, in both instances, violated with abandon—ostensibly in pursuit of a cause that never had, or quickly lost, any semblance of popular appeal. Corruption and cronyism eroded the effectiveness, popularity and legitimacy of regimes in Ghana, Tanzania, Nigeria, Argentina and Brazil. Besides the lack of credibility, an asset that the inept dictatorships—which waxed and now seem to have waned in much of Africa and Latin America—lacked was Japan.[14] As the Japanese started making their presence felt in foreign markets, the ascendancy in world affairs enjoyed by the Western powers was seen to be threatened. Barely two decades after rising from the rubble to which their cities had been reduced, the Japanese had shown they could challenge the West again as they had once done in routing Russia early in the century. Not only were they successfully taking on the industrial nations, but they were doing so with the latter's own weapons! Domestic savings were being invested, foreign technology licensed and "borrowed," imports restricted and management techniques adopted and adapted. So what if the Japanese producer prospered and the consumer suffered by paying higher prices than those prevailing abroad? Short-term sacrifices were worth making if they led to a stronger country, a goal toward which everyone devoutly aspired. So what if the principle of comparative advantage was employed selectively? The scales have been tilted against us for so long that it is now our turn to use what leverage we can. So what if our free market is different from your free market? *Your* consumers benefit, and *you* get a strong ally, to boot. Some such apocryphal exchange might well have played itself out in the minds of governmental gurus and decision makers among Japan's neighbors, while ruminating on their parlous economic condition and seeking a way out of it. What better role model than Japan, particularly a Japan that seemed to be outdoing the once-invincible Americans and Europeans at their own game, even going so far as to bend or (brazenly) break the rules.

Why weren't Japan's temerity and the emulation it elicited from South Korea and Taiwan nipped in the bud? Myopia or generosity? A bit of both.

Myopia because Japan was not initially viewed as a potential economic power, its customers' purchasing power was not expected to rise appreciably in the near future and immediate payment for technology was often valued over potentially larger profits down the road. Generosity kicked in later. Once the nature of the government-business alliance and the policy role assumed by the Ministry of International Trade and Industry (MITI) became apparent, voices of corporate dissatisfaction were raised in the United States but were generally disputed or ignored by their government. We cannot violate the concept and practice of free trade, they were reminded. Raising trade barriers would only result in retaliations back and forth, which could only work to the detriment of all parties involved. Crafting an industrial policy as MITI was doing was debated but rejected as contravening free enterprise principles. But as significant and perhaps valid justifications as any offered for "going easy" on Japan and its imitators were their location and their political importance.[15] The Soviet Union and

China seemed intent, soon after the Second World War, on expanding their list of client states. The conflict on the Korean peninsula was proof of this objective, if any were needed. Japan, which was not allowed to build up its military capabilities—according to the terms of its Constitution drafted during the Occupation—had to be defended and strengthened. What better way to do this than to ensure that it became an economically robust and productive society? Japan was, so to speak, cut a lot of slack because of the trepidation with which the potential for communist expansion in Asia was viewed. The domino theory was, indeed, validated, but not in the sense it was intended or formulated. Even though Vietnam succumbed to communism—from whose predations it is gradually recovering by a self-administered dose of (surprise!) capitalism—the ideology never really caught fire in Asia, with the possible exception of its neighbors in Indo-china. Rather, the notion of growing capitalism from statism spread like wildfire. Protected by the West, particularly the United States, most of the countries of East and Southeast Asia were free to be inward-looking, focusing on the growth of their economies and on nation building instead of diverting large chunks of their budgets to defending themselves against external threats. Korea in particular, Taiwan to a lesser extent and, later, Malaysia, Thailand and Indonesia have adopted their version of Japanese free enterprise. Japanese investments in the latter three countries have no doubt played a part in persuading them to treat Japan as their mentor. Regardless of how and why this came about, the fact remains that much of Asia seems to have taken a leaf out of Japan's economic and industrial policy manual. Both China and India, all talk of market reforms notwithstanding, are embarked on a course similar in philosophy, if not in detail.

It is now all very well to decry Western ideals, economic principles and even morality, but that is, in fact, an act of heroic amnesia. The forbearance accorded by the West to actions by Asian firms and governments, while no doubt self-serving, was equally clearly integral to the later success of these firms and countries. For instance, in the face of incontestable evidence that Matsushita was dumping televisions in the United States in the 1970s, proceedings were not initiated against the offending firm. Tight restrictions on the inflow of materials and the entry of firms from abroad have been in effect in Japan, South Korea and Taiwan. These countries, in turn, have used the surpluses generated by their exports and from sealed-off domestic markets to undercut competitors abroad (even dumping components such as chips, which Japan and South Korea have been wont to do), as well as to invest in other Asian countries, in Europe and in the United States. Japan, Korea and Taiwan most notably have invested quite heavily in the rest of Asia, Japan being the pioneer in this regard. Taiwan has, of late, poured capital into Thailand and Malaysia. Surpluses generated by exporting to the developed countries have, in effect, been used to finance investments in developing Asia—whose exports to the United States and Europe lead to further surpluses![16]

CAPITALIST CHAMELEONS

The United States has to recognize that a new business system has been spawned and is spreading through Asia, challenging its hegemony just as surely as did the Soviet Union during *its* heyday. No doubt, in dealings with sovereign countries, one cannot dictate or perhaps even suggest how they should organize their affairs, but in a supposedly interdependent world, government-driven nationalist policies masquerading as free enterprise must be acknowledged for what they are—a valiant, if duplicitous, attempt to have one's cake and eat it, too. The World Trade Organization (WTO) and Asia Pacific Economic Cooperation (APEC) provide instruments by which double standards can be moderated. But so long as national goals, often pursued at the expense of one's own people, are accorded primacy, and governments feel free to employ whatever methods they choose to achieve these goals, global interdependence will remain only a mantra. It is, indeed, ironic that a country—Japan—whose firms made customer satisfaction their watchword and their raison d'être should callously collude with its government to overcharge its own domestic consumers. Nevertheless, that, in effect, is what happened. It appears that Japan has spawned a horde of ardent followers who espouse a similar ideology. One way to defuse this potentially volatile situation is by making an example of Japan. The United States—and several European countries, to a lesser degree—has tried to get the Japanese to open their markets, using a range of methods that have included cajoling, bargaining and hectoring. The Structural Impediments Initiative (SII), for instance, covered all these but yielded little fruit. True, Motorola gained greater access, and American auto parts are likely to be more easily available in Japan, but this is no more than the tip of the protectionist iceberg. I am reminded of a tale told about a mother who, on inquiring about her son's progress at school, was informed that he was a troublemaker and seemed to be inciting others to follow him. The mother thought for a while and replied: "Johnny is a very sensitive boy. If you have to discipline him, just punish someone sitting near him, and he'll get the message!" The numerous slaps on the wrist that Japan has received are not going to intimidate its Asian coconspirators and have made one thing clear—selective or one-way free enterprise works. Weak Western protests only serve to encourage cheating. Of course, the variations introduced into the operation of the market model by Asian nations call for a spirit of dedication, either intrinsically or extrinsically generated, on the part of the people concerned, patience and the willingness to save and governmental perspicuity, as well as the emergence of companies and corporate leadership capable of giving shape and substance to the policies envisioned. Moreover, each country in Asia hopeful of emulating Japan's meteoric rise has fine-tuned its own policy framework starting from a foundation of government guidance and control. South Korea, unlike Japan, cheerfully canvassed foreign investment but (like Japan) did not, and does not, welcome foreign firms to its shores. China, which, according to some observers, is following the South Korean model, has, however, not only welcomed foreign money but also encouraged firms from abroad to establish production facilities within the country. Both Japan and South Korea effected their remarkable turnaround through the growth of their large corporations. In Japan, small and medium enterprises (SMEs) are partners and play a supporting role, while in Korea SMEs are dysfunctional and a cause for concern. In China, foreign firms, primarily ones based in Hong Kong, and Taiwan have led the charge. In fact, the economic rise of modern China can be attributed, in large part, to investments and technology imported into the mainland by the expatriate Chinese. The latter have also been instrumental, in no small part, for the rising prosperity experienced by Malaysia, Indonesia and Thailand, even if it be to the consternation of the powers-that-be in the former two nations.[17]

On the face of it, most Asian economies will continue to double in size every decade or so, with a concomitant rise in employment levels and quality of life. Given that growth rates in most industries are likely to parallel and, in some cases exceed the growth rate of the economy, MNCs are understandably likely to invest in these attractive markets, contributing even more momentum to their expansion. Are we, in truth, witnessing the dawn of a Pacific century? Can we announce, along with the end of history, the end of the West as well? Should people living in North America and Western Europe start learning Japanese, Korean, Chinese, Hindi or Malay?

MORE OF THE SAME WILL NOT BE ENOUGH

Of course, it's always a good idea and an adventure of sorts to learn a new language. When it's the language of a part of the world that is achieving industrial prominence and accumulating wealth in leaps and bounds, one doesn't have to be a genius to figure out the advantages of doing so. But the day is nowhere in sight when Asian countries—apart from Japan—are likely to be exercising the degree of influence on their erstwhile colonists that the latter once wielded. Such a reversal of fortune, though not in the cards anytime soon, is undeniably a conclusion many Asian countries devoutly desire. It is obviously a powerful motivator to believe that one can get even with one's former oppressor(s), and nations that have felt the colonial lash are driven by more than an internal fire. Malaysia and India have a British colonial past, Indonesia's is Dutch, much of Indochina was under the French and China had many foreign powers (including Japan) occupying parts of it at different times in the past century, while the Philippines was once a part of the Spanish Empire and, later, an American protectorate. In much of Asia, the resentment toward the former overlord has been at least partly transmuted to racial animosity. Unstated though it may be, the rhetoric (sometimes shrill and aggressive) employed to criticize the West, particularly the United States, stems from Caucasian nations having been the dominant world powers of the past four centuries. No matter how cordial relations between Asian and Western countries become, race will continue to be a divisive factor. It is, in fact, a problem within Asia as well. It is no secret that the Japanese consider themselves inherently superior to their neighbors, a conviction that was all too evident during their occupation of Korea, their brutality in their Chinese campaigns (starkly highlighted by the rape of Nanjing) and their wartime behavior in Southeast Asia. The Japanese, though still distrusted, particularly in Korea and China, have attempted to make amends. In a variation of the early Christian practice of buying indulgences, they have assiduously worked at spending their way out of the doghouse. In countries like Malaysia, Indonesia and Thailand, Japanese investments have made a palpable contribution to rising affluence and industrial capabilities.[18] More recently, China has been the object of their attentions, though the expatriate Chinese have contributed far more to the flood of money and ideas into their old homeland than anyone else. Of course, the Japanese have not been forking out their hard-won yen solely to demonstrate penitence or altruism. They have established centers of low-cost manufacturing for themselves in countries like Malaysia and Thailand, from which products the Japanese used to make are shipped to Japan or elsewhere. The complex assemblies and sophisticated production equipment still come from—you guessed it! Dislike for the white former colonists is further compounded by the fact that some countries (e.g., Malaysia) feel they have reached their present status without appreciable Western investment or technology, and others (e.g., China) realize that Western companies are after their burgeoning markets, clearly a mutually beneficial arrangement. The racial antipathy, therefore, continues, and even much of the heat generated over human rights has to be viewed against this backdrop. When an Asian leader proclaims that democracy and the rights of the individual are Western concepts, incongruous in an Asian setting, he or she is asserting the firm conviction that Western countries belong to a race that once dominated the world and need to recognize that their day in the sun is drawing to a close. In making way for their former colonies and vassals, they must realize that theirs is a failed political system. Obviously, a once powerful race will not relinquish its hold easily, and one has to be watchful against its wiles. Visions of a triumphant East dance in the mind's eye of many, if not all, Asian leaders. If wishes were horses. . . .

One factor that makes all notions of Asian (apart from Japan) ascendancy or even equality little more than a chimera is that much of the success attained by Asian countries (and this includes Japan) has been launched from foreign demand and capabilities. True, countries like Japan, Taiwan, Malaysia and China have shown the acumen to sniff out products needed in large markets, reward exporters for their efforts, encourage foreigners, when necessary, to invest domestically, permit imports in the interest of generating more exports and so on. They have shown the finesse required to keep customers abroad satisfied by modifying designs and production processes as needed to keep up with customers' changing desires and fancies. But the fact remains that rising standards of living have been achieved because the climb started from an extremely low level, and it was in the interest of foreign buyers (attracted by lower prices) and investors (seeking higher returns) to facilitate the rise.[19] As costs rise in the erstwhile low-wage areas, and as other low-cost regions begin to take their place, comparative advantages evaporate. New products and markets must be found *before* the old ones become unviable. Higher value-added products (and services) based on enhanced knowledge and technology levels are typically the direction to take, but this is often a crowded, jostling field to enter and one, moreover, that calls for ever-increasing investments in industries with experienced rivals. Korean firms' investments in semiconductors, for instance, initially helped them make a big splash on the world stage, but it has been a tough haul staying ahead or even keeping up with their Japanese, American and European competitors. Of course, if one is fortunate enough to have a large home market (e.g., Japan, China, India) that can be declared "off-bounds" in select areas, the risks diminish somewhat. But even for countries endowed with ample internal demand, the prognosis is not all favorable. Embarking on conquests abroad while building a fortress around one's possessions cannot work indefinitely—or can it? The Japanese undoubtedly took that route and have equally clearly succeeded in ratcheting their technological and international networking capabilities ever higher. If the Japanese can do it, why not the Chinese, Indians, Indonesians and anyone else who can implement a similar asymmetric trade regime? Well, for one, you cannot take people by surprise more than once unless they're gullible or stupid. The eagerness of MNCs to invest abroad notwithstanding, Western nations are, to say the least, wary of Eastern intentions. As Korea is discovering, even with generous dollops of Japanese technology, "doing" another Japan is uphill work. Not only are the playing conditions getting more taxing, with Western firms implementing higher-quality and more efficient production processes, but the old rules are also being reformulated; for example, reciprocal market access is increasingly being demanded as the price for selling and investing in developed countries. At least as worrisome are the emergence of multiple alternative destinations for Western (and Japanese) capital and the rise of numerous low-cost manufacturing locations, most of them seeking foreign markets for their goods, all of them aspiring to climb the ladder of technological self-sufficiency and, perhaps, even innovation. Can China, India or Indonesia follow in Japan's footsteps or, as some scholars point out, successfully and persistently distort the equation of international trade in their favor, as Britain and the United States did during their rises to respective eminence? While the Japanese example is difficult to emulate for the reasons indicated earlier, the likelihood that the conditions accompanying the sequential rise of the Anglo-American powers can be replicated is even more remote. Though both Britain and America did, indeed restrict entry to their own markets, while exporting value-added products and importing only raw materials (e.g., Indian cotton textile were kept out of the English market in order to keep the looms in Lancashire spinning), they had the military power either to enforce their policies abroad or to (externally) protect their domestic industry.[20] Neither country achieved high rates of economic growth through the satisfaction of, and dependence on, foreign consumers. Their own consumers came first, and both countries' writ ran large because their power was based on domestic industry and articulated through offensive (British) or defensive (American) weaponry.

Apart from the varied external reactions—ranging from hostility, to praise and imitation—other questions linger over whether or not Asia's economic ascent can be sustained. Doubts over Asia's future's being an extrapolation of its present and immediate past center around the familiar issues of technology, science, management, culture—the various capabilities and characteristics of a society that define it and provide a measure of its potential. Clearly, countries like Japan, South Korea, Taiwan and Singapore are far from being technological neophytes. Electronics, composite materials, biotechnology—you name it, and these countries have instituted, or are instituting, measures to enhance their competence, narrow the gap with developed nations and, more recently, stake their own claims to being innovators. Even relative newcomers to the economic growth race like China are planning on doubling their research and development intensity (R&D as a percentage of GDP) by the turn of the century. Subsidies to businesses, encouragement of technology-rich joint ventures, the establishment of service and technology parks and governmental involvement in all stages of the research and development process have helped accelerate absorption, diffusion and communication of know-how and know-why. But despite all the laser, rocket and genetic wizardry, the jury is still out on Asia's scientific and technological capabilities. The fact is that Asian advancement had been along the lines charted by their American and European mentors. Even Japan, whose R&D spending per capita matches that of the United States—this following a cold war period during which the United States spent nearly a third of its R&D dollar on defense—has yet to demonstrate that its technical achievements match its efforts. South Korea, Taiwan and Singapore, their technological heroics notwithstanding, have not established an independent standing in this arena. Until they do so, following in the West's footsteps will not serve as the most convincing demonstration of competence in original research. Successful, commercially focused (applied) research and the development of more efficient manufacturing processes (at both of which the Japanese have excelled, and their Asian imitators seem to do reasonably well) are profitable and help in stealing markets from one's rivals, but they are hardly the stuff of which world product or service leadership is made.

Even more glaring are Asian deficiencies in management. This might appear to be an outrageous statement to make considering all the adulation heaped on Japanese firms for their ability to improve productivity and quality and to empower and motivate employees. If, for the moment, we ignore Japan, management in the rest of Asia does not inspire great confidence. Businesses are either family-controlled (as in the countries of the Chinese diaspora and in India), past or present creatures of the state, foreign-inspired or run, or given sweetheart deals at home. Of course, for countries emerging from the shadows of backwardness, autarky and political inhibition, the process of developing an indigenous and modern system of management must be slow. The gradual shift to viable management styles by countries like India, China, Taiwan, South Korea and Indonesia to best suit the needs of society can only delay the process of catch-up even more. Until Asian countries find and articulate their own unique ways of structuring organizations, making decisions and motivating employees, they will not be in a position to sustain the growth of science and technology, fend off the entry or avoid the stifling embrace of foreign firms or leave the friendly confines of their home country to do battle abroad. Though intra-Asia trade is rising, and companies from a few Asian countries (in addition to Japan) have started operations abroad (South Korea and Taiwan come to mind), managing firms in unfamiliar, perhaps hostile environs calls for a robust, yet flexible, management system. Even Japan's vaunted multinationals have shown their vulnerability abroad. Nurtured in a homogeneous culture, they have proved to be insensitive, secretive and rigid. They have also been far from infallible in their strategies. Though strategic mistakes are not unique to Asian firms, the attitudes underlying strategic thinking are natural outcomes of the inward-looking, hierarchic, clannish and centripetal tendencies common to most Asian businesses.

Putting management on a more systematized, yet flexible, footing will not come easily, given the cultural and social milieu in which Asian firms operate. This might seem like another outrageous statement to make when one considers the rich praise showered on Asians' work ethic, frugality, saving habits, family loyalties, discipline, self-reliance and a host of associated virtues. Cracks are, however, beginning to appear in the fabric of many Asian societies. These fissures are likely to widen and cause greater concern as the countries of the region start tasting and expecting the fruits of material success. The lure of technology, the pathologies of industrial society and urbanization and the tendencies to collectivism and incremental innovation could erode, insidiously and in tandem with each other, the foundations of Asia's success. In fact, signs that the East is not immune to the West's failings have already started appearing in the form of rapidly rising divorce rates, drug usage, the spread of diseases like AIDS and so on.

This book expands upon the broad theme that Asian growth cannot be extrapolated indefinitely into the future. Building on the thesis that total factor productivity (TFP), the ratio of an economy's outputs to its inputs, has barely risen in Asia's "miracle economies," Krugman, Young and others have argued that there is no indication yet that Asian countries can sustain their growth indefinitely or even into the next century.[21] All the available evidence suggests that the incredible increases in GDP witnessed in the countries of the region, the World Bank's pronouncements to the contrary notwithstanding, are almost entirely attributable to increases in inputs—labor and capital in particular—carefully marshaled and stimulated by the state.

In the succeeding chapters of this book I attempt, in a sense, to expand upon the total factor productivity-based skepticism of Asian achievement. I am not jumping on the bandwagon. There is no discernible bandwagon unless it is for the contention (contrary to mine) that nothing can come between Asia and its destiny of world dominance. I am merely trying to restore a semblance of balance to the debate and to speculations on the question of quo vadis, Asia? Diverging from the economists' preoccupation with quantitative, macrolevel analysis, I deal at length with the factors underlying the TFP deficiency apparently afflicting the Asian continent and expand upon why it would be difficult, perhaps insuperably so, to remedy the ailment.

Some of the euphoria surrounding Asia has, in recent months, started evaporating due in part to the financial crises that have hit countries such as Thailand and Malaysia. Most observers, however, seem to view the malaise as being superficial and temporary.[22] This book takes a different position. Asian deficiencies, it is argued, are systemic and deep. Much more than cosmetic surgery is needed to address the structural problems confronting the region.

NOTES

1. Paul Krugman, in "The Myth of Asia's Miracle," *Foreign Affairs* 73, No. 6 (November–December 1994), argues that Singapore's rise and even that of the other three "paper" tigers (Hong Kong, Taiwan, South Korea) may be traced to input increases. Similar doubts attach to China (the veracity of whose statistics he questions) and to Japan given its apparently permanent slowdown.

2. Alwyn Young provides extensive data to support the thesis that TFP has increased, at best, marginally even in countries like South Korea. "The Tyranny of

Numbers: Confronting the Statistical Realities of the East Asian Growth Experience," *The Quarterly Journal of Economics* 110, No. 3 (1995): 641–80 illustrates the low productivity increases in Asia, the complexity involved in calculating TFP and the need to dig deeper to better understand why the rate of increase has not been any steeper.

3. See, for instance, *The Coming Conflict with China* (New York: Knopf, 1997), in which Richard Bernstein and Ross Munro convincingly build a thesis of rising uncertainty in Asia occasioned by a confident, powerful China. The threat of instability looms so large that more will—in fact, must—be said on this subject later.

4. South Korea's "condensed" growth (i.e., accelerated catch-up within the span of one generation) is well captured in Cho Soon's *The Dynamics of Korean Economic Development* (Washington, D.C.: Institute for International Economics, 1994).

5. The World Bank's report, *The East Asian Miracle* (New York: Oxford, 1993), delineates this variation in technology orientation clearly (p. 21).

6. A brief overview of the Philippines' efforts in this direction is provided by Peter Waldman's report in the *Wall Street Journal*, October 4, 1996.

7. The political and market factors powering China's rise are detailed in William Overholt's *The Rise of China* (New York: W. W. Norton, 1993), which provides an informative, if uniformly complimentary, perspective on the country's policies and achievements.

8. Ibid.

9. Even five years after the so-called market reforms were introduced, India still seems to exhibit the social-political-cultural-economic multiple personality that got it into the mess in which it found itself in mid-1991. A recent *Wall Street Journal* report (from Miriam Jordan, June 6, 1996) underscores the long road ahead.

10. *The World in 1997* (London: The Economist, 1996), p. 71.

11. *The Economist*, January 14, 1995.

12. The view that economic growth and national security are inseparable was articulated by the government soon after the Second World War ended. Clyde Prestowitz's *Trading Places* (New York: Basic Books, 1988) paints an informative, if colorful, picture of the Mandarins and their strategies (pp. 110–50).

13. World Bank, *The East Asian Miracle*.

14. The Japanese influence on the rest of Asia and their investments in the continent are incontestable. Jim Rohwer's *Asia Rising* (New York: Touchstone, 1995) offers evidence of this phenomenon.

15. Prestowitz, *Trading Places*.

16. Lester Thurow's *The Future of Capitalism* (New York: Penguin, 1996) argues that this cannot continue indefinitely. The U.S. budget deficit will at some time cause sufficient concern to start reducing the trade deficit.

17. World Bank, *The East Asian Miracle*.

18. See Thurow, *The Future of Capitalism*.

19. See William Greider's *One World, Ready or Not* (New York: Simon and Schuster, 1997).

20. James Fallows' contention is that Japan and the rest of Asia are merely practicing what the European economist List propounded and what Britain and the United States had done earlier in their histories.

21. See Krugman, "The Myth of Asia's Miracle"; Young, "The Tyranny of Numbers."

22. Among other respected publications, *The Economist* and the *Wall Street Journal* have expressed concern at the recent turn of events. See, for instance, *The Economist*, August 16, 1997, and the *Wall Street Journal*, October 6, 1997.

2

States Strong and Helpless

Few will argue with the proposition that Japan served first as role model and source of moral support to the struggling nations of Asia (e.g., South Korea and Taiwan) in the 1960s and 1970s, later developing into a direct investor and even technological mentor.[1] While the Japanese are not remembered fondly anywhere in Asia for their military exploits, aggression and ruthlessness, they did undoubtedly point the way to the rest of a pragmatic continent. They not only adopted the prevailing economic system in the West but adapted it to their needs and turned it to their advantage in a race to outdo their vanquishers in the Second World War. There is little doubt that Japan's *kohutai*, or national will, was firmly set, in the days following the country's defeat, on the recovery of its lost position and prestige as the premier power in the continent. The American desire to rebuild Japan, the benevolent nature of the Occupation and the Constitution-mandated minimal-defense stance also contributed to the version of capitalism that has evolved in Japan over the past half century.

Origins apart, the sharp cleavage between Japanese capitalism and the Anglo-American version is quite obvious. The big difference, as even the most casual observer will point out, has been the active and almost passionately partisan role played by the government. The part-bitter, part-sardonic characterization of Japan's system as "chameleon capitalism" is appropriate, perhaps, in more ways than originally intended. The Japanese version of capitalism changed its color, for instance, by encouraging intense competition in certain industries (e.g., television) while initiating cartelization in others (e.g., aluminum).[2] The inherently deceptive nature of the system is exemplified by its practicing one regimen at home (i.e., restricting the entry of foreign firms) while exploiting market opportunities abroad.

The link between the intent to deceive and the predatory behavior of a package of Japanese institutions acting in concert needs little elaboration. If one takes the parallel to ecology a step further, some interesting conclusions emerge. Having sharpened their survival skills at home—where they were not distracted or troubled by the entry of firms (species) from other lands—firms (species) from Japan developed certain capabilities (incremental product development and continuous process improvement) essential for survival at home and deployed these capabilities while doing battle abroad. These "niche" abilities helped achieve footholds leading to eventual dominance in a string of industries ranging from shipbuilding, to semiconductors, from automobiles, to automation. But, given that the Japanese have been spending about as much as the United States per capita on R&D since the early 1980s, nearly all of it in the private sector—unlike the United States, which, until the cold war ended, spent nearly one-third of its R&D dollars on defense[3]—the achievement of technological leadership still eludes them, except in narrowly specified areas. Will the Japanese always remain niche competitors? Will they always remain a "niche country" (i.e., a country whose only impact on the rest of the world is economic and for whose political, religious and cultural direction one must look elsewhere)? These and other such questions relating to the future of Japanese and, indeed, Asian institutions are considered in later chapters.

The role of the Japanese government has been described variously as that of a "strong state," "developmental state" and "catalytic state."[4] These appellations are worth studying in some detail since they help explain Japan's success (and the success of most other Asian nations), and the discipline needed to achieve it and, ironically, define the very limits of that success. The strong state is essentially one that is relatively united both in the formulation and in the implementation of policies, whatever those policies might be. Interest groups, if they exist, do not have the power to intervene to benefit themselves, nor is the bureaucracy open to diversion of resources to rent seekers under the guise of fulfilling policy guidelines. Obviously, governments must *believe* that their intervention and stern supervision are critical to the economic improvements they seek for the nation. Equally obviously, the strong state is not necessarily synonymous with an authoritarian regime. Japan, for instance, was not a dictatorship during its economic ascent during the postwar years, the homogeneity of its population and their almost consensual support of national goals making for a strong state without coercion. Countries such as Indonesia and Malaysia, on the other hand, while being presided over by far more autocratic regimes than Japan, do not quite fit the bill since, at various times, they have tended to favor certain segments of the population or were co-opted by a powerful, albeit industrious, elite.[5] The epitome of profits and of the state itself—being captured by an elite—was, of course, the Philippines. "Booty capitalism,"[6] as it has been termed, is an all too familiar result of authoritarian

Figure 2.1
State Intervention: A Typology

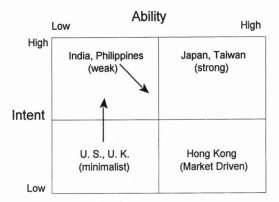

states' serving the interests of powerful patrons. India, on the other hand, over the half century since independence from the British was achieved in 1947, has been a society and polity caught in the cross fire of diverse special interests segmented on the basis of income, caste, region and language. India and the Philippines exemplify the weak state—one that would like to intervene beneficially but succeeds only in filling the coffers of rent-seeking groups with little spillover to the rest of the economy or society. That both these nations are trying to become more market-oriented and reduce their interventionist forays as well as their excessive government expenditures demonstrates a welcome realization of their past ineffectiveness and present reality. All the states mentioned earlier have, in their own manner, *intended* to become developmental states, that is, to achieve accelerating economic growth rates and to permanently alter the context and structure of industrial activity. Only the strong states managed to attain developmental status, not only because they were successful (as, for instance, Chalmers Johnson would have it[7]) but also because they secured prior societal commitment to, or imposed their policies on, their various constituencies, while minimizing or brooking no opposition. The intent to intervene is, therefore, not automatically followed by the ability to do so, as Figure 2.1 illustrates.

STATE INTERVENTION

The United States and Britain have typically tended to adopt minimalist positions, though the United States during the cold war and even in its aftermath, and Britain during its colonial heyday spent heavily on arming themselves, the one ostensibly to defend itself and its allies against the communist threat, the other to project its (primarily naval) power abroad to enforce conformity to the trading regimen it had devised. In general, however, governmental ventures into the market's domain are considered taboo and, worse, in bad taste in the Anglo-Saxon view of the world.[8] Covertly helping defense contractors such as Boeing improve their position in the civilian aircraft industry, bailouts of Lockheed and Chrysler and the imposition of voluntary export restraints (VERs) on Japanese auto imports are aberrations to the minimalist position generally adopted. In fact, most such initiatives undertaken by the government in minimalist countries are hardly subtle, nor do they serve to stimulate the growth of industry. Minimalist countries stand in stark contrast to weak states, which have the intent to encourage and aid domestic business but do not have the wherewithal, the unified will, to do so. It is interesting to note that countries in both the minimalist and weak conditions appear to be shifting their positions gradually. The United States and Britain, for instance, particularly during the latter half of the 1990s, demonstrated their intention to help business. Witness President Clinton's overtures to the Chinese, the administration's efforts at prying open the Japanese market for companies like Kodak and Motorola and the wave of mergers in industries as diverse as entertainment and aircraft manufacturing.[9] The dispatch of numerous trade delegations by Britain to India and the sharp rise in British investment in that country in the 1990s appears to signify a desire on the part of the British government that British multinationals not be left behind in the race for a potentially lucrative market—as they were when the Chinese market reforms first started over a decade earlier. The Indians and the Filipinos, on the other hand, appear to have realized the error of their respective dirigiste and plutocratic ways, freeing and opening up markets progressively. The shift in government policy is, optimistically, directed toward a completely hands-off approach, but, as can be surmised from a cursory look at the postwar trajectories of their countries, visions of government-as-benefactor, on one hand, and of the elites as prime beneficiaries of economic growth, on the other, die hard. Progress has been, and will continue to be, slow, though the cause of equity in the Philippines might turn out to be less intractable than the detachment, albeit gradual, of government from the market process in erstwhile socialist India.

Amid these illustrations of the government's very visible hand in the market process stands Hong Kong, a role model for those states that wish to retire gracefully to the sidelines. One must recognize, of course, that Hong Kong has enjoyed and exploited a unique position in the annals of development. Initially an entrepot port, Hong Kong was in the forefront of Asia countries to make adjustments to succeed in what is now almost a truism—the global economy. Light engineering and low-end manufacturing undertaken in factories harking back to the sweatshops of an earlier European time and the need to export—given the limited market capacity of the island—initially to their equally impecunious neighbors in Southeast Asia but later to the United States and Europe, helped propel Hong Kong's economy upward.[10] Subsequent Japanese investment in manufacturing and a laissez-faire financial system gave sustenance to a healthy and now booming stock market. Peculiarities of Hong Kong's antecedent and contemporaneous conditions make emulation of its success difficult. The availability of a steady supply of immigrant labor, the proximity to China's raw material supply and the ability to be a window and reexport center for the mainland, compact size and so on combined to make Hong Kong a relatively inimitable success. Even Singapore needed significant guidance from its governing politicians and bureaucrats in achieving a comparable boom. Whether or not Hong Kong can retain its relatively pristine economic purity, shrugging off the warm embrace of a regime that has rarely been averse to mixing its own cocktail of politics and economics, remains to be seen.

A rather different concern faces Japan and the host of imitators it has spawned, each striving to out-Japan its neighbor. The question that has to be addressed by most Asian countries is, Having come thus far with the active support of an encouraging, collaborative, perhaps generous state, what will happen without, or with less, governmental backing in the years ahead? As developed countries become increasingly alarmed over the loss of jobs and of viability in a range of industries, as the WTO regime begins to take hold and as MNEs increasingly make inroads into hitherto closed markets, can governments continue to favor and assist their own firms? Kenichi Ohmae, in his *The Borderless World* and *The End of the Nation State*,[11] argues that the liberal democratic invention we call the nation-state is withering away, and taking its place are extra-national entities and loyalties. More on this and related subjects later. First, we take a closer look at how government policy and action in Japan helped *this* nation-state get where it is.

One of the most obvious differences between Japan and a dirigiste economy such as that of France is that the government share of the GDP is lower in the former. Though a strong state, Japan's government spends less per capita than do even its counterparts in capitalistic Britain or the United States.[12] Having neither invested as much (per capita) in terms of equity as France nor spent as much as the United States, Japan might be qualified to lay unquestioned claim to being the least interventionist. But, clearly, expenditures or investments do not tell the whole story. They do not even begin to tell the story where Japan is concerned, for the Japanese have risen to prominence not by cultivating the heavy-handed methods of the French or by spending heavily in "unproductive" areas like pollution control or a burgeoning bureaucracy. Rather, they have attempted to (successfully) persuade, influence or just coerce private companies into acting in accord with the direction set by the government. A predictable polity, public acceptance of, and compliance with, the overarching national goal of recovering lost prestige and glory, a stable economic order and a culture that encouraged learning from abroad while rejecting the foreigner have undoubtedly contributed to the ability to gain the utmost cooperation—dare I say subservience?—of corporate strategy to national needs. The fact remains, however, that this convergence of ends and means clearly worked to the benefit of all parties concerned in Japan, resulting in a system that placed firms in the West, unaided, ignored or even penalized (e.g., in terms of regulations regarding pollution, workplace safety etc.) by their home governments, at a distinct disadvantage vis-à-vis their Japanese rivals when the latter emerged from their sequestration in the 1970s.[13]

In truth, Japanese governments have formulated, and continue to formulate, national strategies much as a firm would. That is, they pick products (ships, motorcycles, automobiles, semiconductors) in which they would like their firms to excel and target the markets (primarily the United States and Western Europe) most likely to import these products. Realizing that a national trade strategy requires a long planning horizon, obviously longer than that demanded at the corporate level, the Japanese government, with all the authority at its command, acted carefully and deliberately to implement its strategy of industry dominance. The steel industry, for instance, was nurtured by a combination of diverse policies—capital was loaned at subsidized rates, deepwater ports were constructed to facilitate raw material receiving and the dispatch of finished steel with minimal throughput times, generous depreciation allowances and foreign exchange allocations were made and so on.[14] To minimize wastage of limited funds, "competitors" were "encouraged" to share resources. Oxygen arc technology, imported by one firm, was, therefore, available to all the firms in the industry. As capacity climbed and rapidly rose above domestic demand, Japanese steel was increasingly exported—a strategy that the government and its co-conspirators in the private sector had envisioned while establishing steel mills producing 10 million tons a year—spelling serious trouble for the inefficient, defenseless mills across the Pacific. The pattern has been similar in industries like televisions, videocassette recorders (VCRs), semiconductors, automobiles and consumer electronics.[15] One has to give the Japanese credit for their ability to make the private sector an *instrument* of trade strategy. Unlike the socio-capitalist states of Europe, Japan's international success, orchestrated as it might have been by the state, devolved around the competitive capabilities of its corporations. True, it helped guard infant industries from foreign competition, regulated the ingress of technology, unless it was licensed to a domestic firm, and denied investment opportunities to foreign firms audacious enough to seek a piece of the growing Japanese market. But the fact remains that protected industries did not become fat and lazy, secure in the knowledge that they were immune to all danger. To the contrary, no such immunity was granted. Companies knew that they had to build the capabilities necessary to survive in the Japanese market and typically, at a later date, compete in export markets. Japan was no autarky. Ideas, though not products and firms, entered relatively freely, a term I use advisedly. Technology was critical to Japanese national strategy, but the price paid for foreign technologies was negligible (e.g., in licensing fees) compared to the lucrative use made of them. Products flowed copiously outward, often incorporating the very technology that had been imported at bargain-basement prices. It is tempting to conclude that all of Japan's success is based on know-how purloined or copied from the West, but that would not be the truth. It would, however, not be far from the truth, since all Japan's triumphs have been achieved in areas pioneered in the West, though one has to admit that they have improved upon what they learned from the respective industry leaders in the United States and Europe. First, MITI has been very active in organizing national research and development projects, so as to minimize resource wastage and sharing of capabilities, in industries such as steel, consumer electronics and semiconductors.[16] The research was, relative to the scale of investment in the industries, no more than marginally subsidized by MITI, but—it certainly bears repeating—effective governmental intervention is best calibrated by its impact, not by how much expenditure is incurred.

Whether it was in enabling companies such as Sony and Matsushita to acquire transistor technology without surrendering market access or in nudging the semiconductor industry toward a vertically integrated structure, MITI pulled the strings, and the firms complied. In the semiconductor industry, for instance, Toshiba and Nippon Electric built capabilities through most of the value chain, manufacturing semiconductors for sale as well as for use in their equipment, covering most component and finished product areas in the computer business. In the United States, on the other hand, the industry has a multilayered structure comprising product firms (e.g., IBM, AT&T), diversified merchant producers of chips (Motorola), companies like Intel that specialize in chips, others that specialize in particular kinds of chips (e.g., Cypress) and makers of chip-making equipment. Fragmentation in the U.S. industry and scale economies in Japanese production (coupled with the possible "dumping" of their chips on world markets) conferred an initial advantage on the integrated firm, a category that later came to include South Korean conglomerates like Hyundai.[17] The American response, though belated, was spirited. Nearly all the firms in the semiconductor industry, upstream and downstream, merchants and users, collaborated in research, development and engineering to recover much of the ground that had been earlier conceded to the Japanese, Koreans and, more recently, Malaysians.[18]

Not everything that MITI touched, however, turned to gold. Subsidies given to coal, textile and petrochemicals—the latter in the years leading up to the Arab oil embargo—were wasted investments. MITI's reluctance to support Sony's entry into the transistor radio business and its attempt to throw cold water on some automobile manufactures' (such as Toyota's) decision to pursue international competitiveness are among two of MITI's best-known snafus. MITI's mistakes notwithstanding, the intent to guide markets is unmistakable. By keeping out foreign competition using a combination of tariffs, subsidies for local firms, preferential purchasing and archaic distribution, MITI gave domestic firms a breathing space during which their investments would not be at risk due to the entry of predatory foreigners. "Excessive competition," seemingly an oxymoron in most capitalistic circles, was deemed to be a danger to free enterprise since its evil twin, overcapacity, could lead firms to engage in suicidal and fratricidal price reductions. Cartels were encouraged or created by MITI for petrochemicals, cement and steel plate, which resulted in premiums for these products of 60, 57 and 48% respectively, over their imported prices.[19] Ironically, a nation whose standard-bearers in the conquest of foreign markets immortalized the slogan "The customer is king" treated its own consumers like anything but royalty. Prices higher than those prevailing in Europe and the United States were routinely paid by Japanese customers, not just for basic materials but for consumer goods both durable and nondurable, as well as for agricultural products. While the reasoning behind limiting competition, domestic and foreign, varied from one sphere to another, the effect was uniformly the same. Consumers were kings only in the international markets, which Japanese corporations sought to make their own. At home, the consumer was being robbed.

In pursuing its producer-first policies, MITI, as we have seen, established a regimen of identifying the industries in which catch-up was needed, based on an evaluation of their potential, interfirm collaboration—which, on occasion, developed into outright collusion—a limiting of excess competition, presenting a united face to the rest of the world and the creation of technopolises, or science and technology parks, to encourage the free exchange and cross-fertilization of ideas among diverse research institutions. MITI's success is demonstrated both by the outstanding performance of its large client firms abroad as well as by the process improvements and unique management systems that these firms introduced and have become famous for. Toyota, Canon and a legion of other Japanese firms might well take umbrage at MITI's getting credit for manufacturing and management innovations to which the corporations concerned could rightfully lay claim. Let me hasten to allow that total quality management, just-in-time (JIT) manufacturing, kaizen, total productive maintenance (and other related, innovative approaches to doing business) were, indeed, uniquely Japanese contributions to modern management. JIT, for instance, represents a frontal assault on the major assumptions attending the origins and growth of the mass production and consumption society. Manufacture in large batches, shop floors overflowing with inventory and a desire to push the product out the door were no longer considered essential to low-cost production.[20] The *kanban* system with its emphasis on set-up time reduction (so that more frequent changeovers caused by increasing product variety caused minimum disruption), worker control over the line and customer demand-driven work flow changed all that. Ostensibly, the Japanese success in their export ventures was a natural outcome of their manufacturing magic combined with an uncanny feel for customers' needs—indeed, a praiseworthy amalgam of capabilities, even more praiseworthy when one recalls how cavalier Japanese firms were to their own consumers at that time.

It might appear to be beyond all debate that Japan's success in foreign markets was due to the nexus of its unique manufacturing philosophy with an unerring sense for customers' needs. However, that's where the strong Japanese state steps in. By "encouraging" banks to lend at low interest rates to large borrowers and to take a benign view of repayment delays, not acting to enforce shareholders' rights, the clear bias toward employers' versus employees' privileges, fostering of cooperation bordering on collusion between firms and keeping out foreign firms while avidly importing/borrowing their technology, Japan not only helped its domestic producers overcome their initial fragility but ensured that predators from abroad would not pick off its infant industries while they were still fledglings. The exchange of threat strategy routinely followed by MNEs—attacking a foreign competitor in its own backyard—was, as a result, closed to American and European firms feeling the sting of imported products. Whether the deterrent took the form of tariffs, prohibitions or industrial structure matters little. The fact remains that the governmental shield gave Japanese producers the breathing space they needed to build up the muscle and fat they needed to take on their unwary, unprotected opponents abroad. The superiority of certain Japanese practices of management cannot be questioned, nor can the government's clear intent to create competitive industries, not sheltered weaklings, be gainsaid. However, self-righteous assertions to the effect that the "natural genius" of the Japanese people was instrumental in their developing pragmatically effective systems of management need to be heavily discounted. Without the cordoning-off, cohesion-inducing actions of the government—MITI in particular—none of it would have been possible.

The Japanese state is sometimes referred to as a "catalytic" one,[21] in the sense that it caused the other protagonists in economic society to alter their behavior while itself remaining unchanged. Nothing could be further from the truth. A long regimen of intervention has left the government addicted, so to speak, to a diet of intervention. It was unwilling to dismantle the entry barriers particularly in industries like auto parts, paper and cellular phones. In the case of the last, when prolonged U.S. government pressure finally pried open the door, Motorola captured around 30% of the market.[22] Paper is still being jealously guarded in spite of an earlier agreement to open it up in 1994. It is neither a nascent industry nor an efficient one and, if it had been in the United States or Western Europe, would have come under attack from Japanese and perhaps Korean firms. Auto parts, we are told authoritatively and with finality, almost entirely consist of *keiretsu* partners, an arrangement that cannot be tinkered with. Strategic alliances are, after all, legitimate sources of competitive advantage, and why should Japanese firms be penalized for establishing relationships that are both legal and effective? The entire issue of so-called network capitalism is dealt with in greater detail in Chapter 5. At this point, suffice it to say that the *keiretsus*, which are linkages of firms based on commonalities of purpose, for example, the customer–supplier relationship buttressed by cross-shareholding, are, in effect, exclusivity clauses. They exercise restraint on whom firms may do business with, which may not seem like an unfair trade—or, for that matter, business—practice. After all, establishing relationships and trust with whomever you do business with is a time-honored recipe for durable success in business dealings. Where networks of suppliers and customers are created, the transaction costs incurred in frequently or even occasionally conducting business with the market can be sharply curtailed. Little wonder that Japanese *keiretsus* and Chinese family networks prefer to continue with existing relationships rather than explore new partners, which has been the accepted practice in the United States. While this seems reasonable enough, the fact remains that it effectively blocks new and, therefore, foreign firms from entering the industry since such a move would necessitate building capabilities in a string of diverse activities, acquiring a host of firms (which is almost as difficult in most Asian countries as building capabilities from the ground up) or entering the industry with a network of one's own—which, obviously, would be little more than wishful thinking. Worse than being exclusive on business-related grounds alone, the various kinds of networks are exclusive on ethnic grounds as well. While at home the question of ethnic exclusivity does not arise, when the *keiretsus* and Chinese businesses venture abroad, they exhibit what I would term, not completely in jest, the "Dracula syndrome." The nocturnal count, according to popular legend, did not travel out of the friendly confines of his native Transylvania without taking along boxes of his native earth. Japanese firms, similarly, are loath to leave their shores without their trusted *keiretsu* partners. Insecurity? Efficiency-driven relationships? Perhaps, but, while operating away from the friendly confines of home, traveling in corporate coteries—especially when little effort is made to locate or nurture local partners—smacks of bias or, worse, ethnic and cultural chauvinism. Suggesting that *keiretsus*—and other forms of Asian networks—are integral to Asian relationship-oriented (in contrast to Western task-oriented) values is a convenient ploy enabling governments to, as the saying goes, "run with the fox and hunt with the hounds"! The state can, generously and frequently, pay lip service to free markets and unfettered competition while, apparently, wringing its hands in despair over an industry configuration that runs counter to its own rhetoric. More, as I said— much more—on this later.

Far from being a catalytic entity, the Japanese state has been an active, in truth, a hyperactive and prominent ingredient in the rise to economic superpower status. It has been completely transformed by its role and is, in fact, unable to see how it has distorted the market and the trading regime to serve its own purpose. To use an analogy from physics, firms from countries such as the United States and Britain still see the world in Newtonian three-dimensional terms, while the Japanese and their legion of imitators have an Einsteinian perspective where space-time is warped in order to allow for the relative nature of time itself. Under certain conditions (in physics, at speeds nearing that of light; in economic terms, doing business in Asian nations), the curved nature of space-time and the distorted terms of trade seem "natural," acceptable to all but the most unreasonable. In truth, Japanese bureaucrats, government officials and businessmen are, by and large, convinced that they are practitioners of the one, true form of capitalism, the proof being the extraordinary success they have enjoyed over the past quarter century. Discussions between American and Japanese trade representatives often end in stalemates precisely because the two sides have such radically divergent models of reality in mind. If Japan had been an isolated case of government-inspired (abetted?) corporate competitiveness, it might have served as an interesting case study, one that succeeded, no doubt, in turning capitalism, as one understood it, on its head. As things have turned out, however, Japan's success has emboldened a variety of imitators to emulate its rise by taking leaves out of its textbook on government-orchestrated strategic trade and technology. There was no pupil more willing or eager than South Korea.

Itself colonized and subjugated by Japan, South Korea in the late 1950s and 1960s was living through an uneasy, watchful peace with its communist sibling to the north. Supported by the military might of the United States and bound to the latter by the blood both—and other—allies had shed in repulsing the communist advance, South Korea was ruled by a series of strongmen. The United States, as it did in other parts of Asia—Taiwan and Indonesia, for instance—and in Latin America, turned a blind eye to the distinctly undemocratic, if not antidemocratic, nature of the regimes enlisted in the fight against communism. The South Korean version of the strong state derived, unlike Japan, not so much from the convergence of the public will and government policy in a desire to catch up with, and best, their former conquerors but through *diktat* and a relatively incorruptible bureaucracy. The question of distributional pressures being exerted by interested groups did not even arise under iron-fisted regimes such as those of Syngman Rhee, General Park or even General Chun.[23] The World Bank bestows fulsome praise on South Korea—and Taiwan, for that matter—for its discipline in encouraging exports while steering clear of a policy of import substitution. The exchange rates were market-based, and, in fact, the success of the Korean and Taiwanese ventures was attainable, according to World Bank analysts, by letting the market do its thing while ensuring macroeconomic stability and investing in primary education.[24] True, Korea, like most other governments in North and Southeast Asia, did create the environment for growth. But to say that, having done that, it just stepped back and let the market take over is like saying oxygen is the reason internal combustion engines work. Many factors contribute to the functioning of the engine, of which oxygen, like gasoline and the ignition system, is necessary, though not sufficient. The creation of a favorable climate for business and the encouragement of export-driven firms were no doubt a significant element in the construction of the Korean economic engine. The state's hand was, nevertheless, both visible and heavy. Protection was employed, for example, to nurture infant industries, which were, in turn, "encouraged" to export. Import restrictions in fledgling industries and outright subsidies to established ones complete the picture of strategic trade deployed by the government. The selective import of technology, while eschewing foreign direct investment (unless it was unavoidable in critical sectors), the targeting of certain industries as high priority, for example, the push to develop an indigenous capability in heavy industry and chemicals, and the preferential treatment accorded the emerging conglomerations (*chaebol*) by offering low interest capital and subsidized bans for technology acquisition all point to a determined strategic technology effort. Although all exports were encouraged and rewarded, those that required building a comparative advantage where none existed *and* proceeded to compete in foreign markets were given the most incentives. Undoubtedly, an optimum amalgam of strategic trade and technology theories was operative in the emergence of South Korea as an economic force.[25] Taiwan, no less than South Korea, was an interventionist state in neo-classical liberal economic clothing.[26] While it was a cut a lot of slack by the United States, the region's hegemon, for reasons similar to those favoring South Korea, the prevailing conditions and adapted policies were modified to suit the country's needs. In addition to subsidizing and rewarding exports, restricting imports through various protective means, facilitating credit in selected industries and directing attention and investment toward newer and better technologies, the Taiwanese state also established state-financed corporations, particularly where capital needs were highest, and private investors not forthcoming. Whereas the *chaebol*, reassured by the government's commitment to stimulate domestic ventures and keep out foreign direct investment, undertook the bulk of the investment in Korea, firms on the scale of the *chaebol* (which, in effect, had been nurtured and sedulously tended by the state) simply did not exist in Taiwan. Whether this was due to the ruling party's reluctance to create a business-rooted power center (dominated by native Taiwanese) or the inherent tendency of Chinese societies toward family-owned, small-scale business, the fact remains that the state in Taiwan became both a direct participant in, and facilitator of, industry by investing heavily both in manufacturing as well as, later, in the development of new technologies through the R&D organizations it has sponsored.[27] True, the monolithic developmental state was not blemish-less—the public sector enterprises favored mainlanders in its employment policies, prominent families were given preferential treatment and the Kuomintang Party owned or was a dominant influence in firms that depended on government largesse for their success. These traces of rent-seeking behavior notwithstanding, the Taiwanese government remained as firmly committed to its developmental goals as were its Japanese and Korean predecessors on the same interventionist path.

As we shift our focus to Southeast Asia, we find a cluster of countries—Malaysia, Thailand, Indonesia and the Philippines being the most prominent—that differ markedly from their northern neighbors in certain respects. Unlike Japan, South Korea and Taiwan, the southern nations are relatively heterogeneous in their population mix, the Chinese minority being particularly significant, in influence if not in numbers. Malaysia also has a significant minority of Indian origin. Governments, therefore, must factor in the distributional implications of any policies they adopt. Maintaining a high level of economic growth may not result in a greater sense of well-being. In fact, if income disparities favoring minorities are maintained or exacerbated, resentment and unrest are likely to bubble over. The substantial Chinese minority in Malaysia and the relatively small Chinese population in Indonesia have both felt a sharp backlash against their dominance of commerce. Race riots and bloodletting ensued, followed by an uneasy truce supervised by a partisan government. After the 1969 violence in Malaysia, the state stepped in with laws favoring locals (bumiputras) in government employment and, later, in the private sector, too. When Chinese family firms found ways to circumvent the so-called new economic policy, the government established its own corporations and instituted a system of licensing. Firms that did not comply with employment regulations would not be granted licenses to function in their industry. As the Chinese shifted to industries like real estate where monitoring was difficult, the state decided to end the shadowboxing and extend an invitation to foreign firms to invest in Malaysia, an action that had been anathema to the trailblazers farther north. Malay aversion to the Chinese far outweighed its desire for self-sufficiency, but foreign firms were loath to expose themselves to the forbidden political risks and economic constraints they discerned. When even free trade zones failed to lure capital from abroad, the government took matters into its own hands by setting up mammoth enterprises in the auto, cement and steel industries. The ruling party got into the act, too, by setting up its own businesses—which served the dual purpose of stimulating growth and filling its own coffers. Malays were placed in charge of nearly all the governmental and party-affiliated undertakings. The whole edifice came crashing down in 1986 and 1987, when the state-owned enterprises

(SOEs) suffered calamitous losses.[28] The whole emphasis dramatically shifted. The government reversed its policy, and foreigners and non-Malays were placed in positions of corporate authority to demonstrate the new commitment to market forces and profit maximization. Fortuitously, the Japanese in particular but the South Koreans, too, and, later, the Taiwanese were looking for low-cost locations to invest their cash hoards. Malaysia now seemed to provide the opportunities *and* the security they craved. While the government continues to build the party's finances through the award of lucrative contracts to party-owned firms—the opposition can do little except watch while the press, muzzled in the public interest, is little more than a sleeping watchdog—foreign investment and technology have helped Malaysia maintain a GDP growth rate in excess of 7% over the past five years. The government, by shrewdly diverting resources toward the creation of indigenous research capabilities, particularly in its most recent success story where Foreign Direct Investment (FDI) is concerned, consumer electronics, is attempting to move Malaysia up the technological ladder, enabling it to keep pace with countries like Taiwan and South Korea. Realizing that it cannot match China and India as low-cost production centers or in terms of market size for consumer goods and industrial products, Malaysia during the 1990s has embarked on an ambitious drive to become a knowledge-intensive economy. In consumer electronics, for instance, the government has succeeded in inducing firms to locate design facilities there. Similarly, for semiconductors, of which Malaysia is the world's third largest producer, absorption of know-how is as prominent a mission as the acquisition of world-class manufacturing capabilities in high-technology areas.

As interventionist, politically partisan and economically discriminatory as the Malaysian government has been, Indonesia has managed to match it step for step and even outdo it in certain respects.[29] Resource-rich like its mainland neighbor, Indonesia parlayed its oil wealth into heavy SOE investments in the 1970s and 1980s, resulting in a sharp cutback in FDI in the 1980s. As commodity prices plummeted in the mid-1980s, the country was forced to seek private investment, with FDI rising to 12% of the total, and local private funds accounting for well over half of all investments. Like Malaysia, Indonesia is heterogeneous in its population, though with a much smaller Chinese minority. Perhaps the minuscule percentage (about 5%) they constitute of the total has rendered employment and contracting laws superfluous, but that has resulted in a Chinese stranglehold on Indonesian business. Though the Chinese are resented and disliked by the Malay majority, they have prospered and achieved even greater economic dominance by keeping the engines of power well lubricated. The ruling coterie, headed by General Suharto, his immediate family and close friends, is the direct and predominant beneficiary of Chinese largesse, some of which, naturally, trickles down into the bureaucracy.[30] Indonesia's ability to leverage an outcast minority's ingenuity to its economic benefit may be praised for its success or condemned for its clientelistic character. The results, however, indicate that the government has played an intimate part in the country's transformation.

Unlike Malaysia and Indonesia, race relations in Thailand have, in recent years, been relatively amicable, partly because the Chinese have displayed the ability to blend in with their surroundings, even to the extent of adopting their names as well as intermarrying. Whether or not the fact that Thailand's majority religion is Buddhism, while that of Malaysia and Indonesia is Islam has anything to do with it is beyond the scope of this discussion. Whatever the reasons might be, the relative ethnic harmony has induced a greater convergence in business and government goals, a higher incidence of lobbying and more pervasive, "egalitarian" corruption.[31] In spite of the widespread corruption, Thailand, too, has averaged remarkable growth rates of around 7% over the last quarter century. Japanese and Taiwanese FDI have no doubt helped create technological capabilities in industries like auto manufacturing. Lately, Thai firms have demonstrated an ability to operate abroad, even in the United States, a relatively rare occurrence among emerging nations. The government has played a less intrusive role in Thailand than in Indonesia or Malaysia and is less protectionist than the government in Japan, Taiwan or South Korea, but there is little doubt that policy has been carefully orchestrated and coordinated among the politicians/military (often synonymous with each other) and bureaucracy, as well as business leaders and industry associations. A word about the Philippines, hitherto one of the poorest countries in Asia, ignored and even scorned by foreign investors. A client state of the United States, the Philippines has been an exponent of what some observers have referred to as "booty capitalism." Government policy has been tailored to earn the maximum possible returns for the ruling elite. Lacking the developmental goals pursued by states such as Thailand, Indonesia and Malaysia and the discipline to subordinate the rent-seeking behavior of powerful groups to the pursuit of national goals—as its Southeast Asian neighbors succeeded in doing—the Philippines fell prey to the avarice of its ruling politicians. In recent years, with wage rates rising in Malaysia and Thailand and an active wooing of foreign investors by the Ramos regime to establish export-driven industries, things are beginning to look up.[32] Subic Bay, for instance, has been designated a special economic zone and is humming with activity. It has often been asserted that the Philippines languished because it was a democracy. In reality, the country was no more a democracy than Indonesia is today. The lack of the desire, ability and will to rise above petty ambitions and persistent cronyism, coupled with an unrepentantly authoritarian regime—which, by no stretch of the imagination, could be labeled democratic—brought this nation of islands to its knees.

After Tiananmen 1989, few will mention democracy and China in the same breath. (Not that the economy has even paused, so to speak, for breath during a period spanning nearly two decades.) The absence of democratic freedoms does not appear to faze foreign investors, local entrepreneurs or the person on the street—high GDP growth rates and rising disposable incomes particularly in the favored southeastern coastal belt, have whetted the popular appetite for market reforms. Just as the absence of political freedom has ostensibly not served as a brake or even cast a shadow over China's headlong economic growth, the existence of democratic institutions has not been the only or even the major factor contributing to India's stagnation until the early 1990s. The freeing of the polity and the stifling of the economy were both done by the same government, which might indicate a schizophrenic bent but reflected, in reality, the belief that the state knew better than any other institution—particularly one as irresponsible as the market—what was best for everyone.

China's post-cultural revolution conversion to capitalist beliefs was neither as miraculous nor complete as one might be disposed to believe, but it certainly was striking. For a country in which all the so-called bourgeoisie and elites (doctors, teachers, engineers, nurses and so on) were fair game for party functionaries and anyone else who resented the relatively well-off for possessing skills and knowledge they themselves lacked, China seemed to be magically transformed into a country anxious to learn and to earn. The transformation was not really abrupt, since the country's leaders, looking for a way out of a morass that had almost swallowed them, decided that opening the door just a crack, in select regions near beehives of economic activity like Hong Kong and Taiwan—both part of the Greater China network—would minimize the risk of a political backlash. Such a backlash was, at any rate highly unlikely, given the revulsion that the people at large had developed for the excesses perpetrated by the Red Guards.[33] Having discovered that degradation of the haves did not benefit the have-nots and faced with mounting evidence that the country was being left in the dust by its neighbors (and erstwhile economic equals), the will and the desire for change had, by 1979, built up an almost irresistible head of steam. The changes initiated by Deng Xiaoping were not complete either, in the sense that some of the shibboleths of traditional communist—of "free-market socialist," as it was termed—ideology were retained. Though private industry was to be the engine of growth, as in any capitalist economy, the government did not, by any means become a bystander. For one, the SOEs, which in the early 1980s provided well over half of the country's GDP and were grossly inefficient, were initially—an attitude that persists today—considered too sensitive to dismantle or even tinker with. The various "iron bowls" (i.e., assurances in regard to jobs, food availability, health and Social Security etc.) were integral to communist rule and continued to occupy the same centrality in the 1980s and 1990s.[34] The government also designated certain areas as special economic zones and provided the infrastructural support needed for FDI-financed ventures, primarily funded by investors in Hong Kong and Taiwan to function effectively. Exports were the prime focus, and, as in countries like South Korea, Taiwan and Malaysia, the government bent over backward by providing all the subsidies and incentives needed to stimulate exports and deter imports. While the government has, by and large, remained firmly in control of the developmental direction taken by the country, it has been compelled to invite foreign capital to jump-start the growth process. The bulk of the FDI has come from expatriate Chinese in Hong Kong and Taiwan, which has reduced the potential for difficulties arising from cultural and ethnic differences between investor and recipient. Much of the growth in China may be attributed to the SEZs while the drag on the country's upward trajectory derives, in the main from a reluctance to take on waste in the SOEs and retract the cradle-to-grave safety net and the desire to control the farthest reaches of the country from Beijing. The state has been a central, dominant figure in the development of China, and, though the government has not always had things its own way—Tiananmen Square 1989 was a reminder of how ambivalence in a government can be tragic, while the increasing autonomy of the provinces gives rise to fears of centripetal forces, a prospect about which all politicians in the central government are paranoid—the fact remains that China has so far followed, with great success, a script selectively borrowed from its Northeastern and Southeastern Asian mentors. As it increasingly begins to write its own script, writing in parts and events its mentor playwrights had not envisioned, it may find itself on less familiar and unpredictable ground.

The state has been as significant an influence in India as it has been in China, though with far more, to put it charitably, uneven results. Import substitution was long a centerpiece of the government's growth plan, coupled with heavy investments in public sector undertakings (PSUs), which drained public resources providing only minuscule returns (if any). Just as in most socialist and communist countries, the government-owned corporations were often monopolistic, charging high prices to customers, who had little recourse and, worse, were often arms of the state themselves.[35] India had the advantage of an active private sector, including in industries like automobiles, medium-capacity electrical equipment, consumer goods, textiles and synthetic fiber and so on. The competitive environment was so highly circumscribed by government regulations, however, that firms could not grow without government benevolence, which, when bestowed, ensured success. Indian firms, therefore, developed great expertise at dealing with the government and little in the area of product/process technology, managerial development and so on. With imports being frowned upon and exports a low priority to most industries (both stemming from government policy initiatives or a lack thereof), foreign benchmarks for performance and methods used were nonexistent and, indeed, irrelevant. Only when the nation almost defaulted on interest payable on its loans in 1991 were the so-called market reforms undertaken. Unlike most other countries in Asia, barring perhaps China, India has to scale down the level of governmental involvement in its economy. The Chinese state has not, across the board, become less active: it has merely exchanged its obstructionist role for a facilitative one. India is attempting to do the same—a mixture of subsidies and incentives is being provided to exporters, while quotas and other restrictions on the output of domestic firms are being reduced or eliminated.[36] Multinationals are being induced to invest in the country by dangling lower tax rates, incentives for transferring technology, higher limits on foreign ownership and so on. Long years of obstructionist behavior have, however, had a corrosive effect on India's bureaucracy, polity and, in general, society at large. The prospect of the government's staying out of market dealings and allowing efficiency considerations to replace it alarms politicians and officials alike, the latter since it would erode their authority, the former since it might loosen the hold they exercise over their voting blocs. A general impression that the market is selfish and inimical to the well-being of the general public—a hangover from the days when anti-imperialist rhetoric was an easy route to popularity—pervades all debates over the relaxation of governmental controls. While most Western countries have grappled with this issue for decades, in India's case, the movement sought is in the reverse direction (i.e., from too much government to progressively more dependence on private initiative, rather than from predominantly private enterprise to state-mandated or-supported public welfare programs), making it essential for the government to communicate the rationale behind its retreat from autarky, favoritism, rigid control and well-meaning incompetence. Even China's abrupt about-face in 1979 was less fraught with uncertainty, since much of the population had had enough of state-inspired political chaos and the accompanying economic collapse. As the government struggles to grow into its role of facilitator, the danger, paradoxically, is that it might do too much and too little, the former in terms of its historical tendency to assume it knows what's best for everyone, the latter in the sense that it might abdicate its responsibility to build a suitable infrastructure and to provide the necessary stimuli—in the form of subsidies, tax holidays and so on—to attract and hold domestic and foreign investments. Caught between the twin divergent needs to modernize and to placate the strong "socialist" interests in its democratic system, India faces the real danger of dithering between policy alternatives and not adopting any with any conviction.

Undoubtedly, India exhibits all the traits of a weak state—a divided polity, an entrenched and often corrupt bureaucracy, SOEs that refuse to shrink appreciably, politicized labor unions and low literacy and high population growth rates. The contrast with countries like Japan, South Korea, Taiwan and even Malaysia, Indonesia, Thailand and China could not be starker. However, there are some silver linings among these seemingly ominous clouds. Skilled labor is plentiful, and the country abounds in engineering and scientific talent, making it an attractive destination for labor-intensive and technology-driven industries such as automobiles and software. The government, in attempting to address the infrastructure deficiencies, has put in place incentives for exporters, is gradually relaxing its draconian grip on private industry and is moving the country toward a consensus on the need for more, not less, capitalism. As in the instance of the Philippines, the culprit behind long years of stagnation is not democracy but wrong-headed government philosophies and actions, and while the jury is still out on India, its movement, though pedestrian and plodding compared to its Asian compatriots and, indeed, rivals, is in the right direction.

What, then, does one make of the government-sparked modernization that has swept through much of the Asian continent? Is it likely to keep up the dizzying pace these nations and their populations have grown accustomed to over the past 25 years? Can the governments of the regions retain control of their various countries and constituencies, while simultaneously charting a course for them at the end of this millennium and the beginning of the next one? Given the changes and discontinuities on the horizon and in the air, the responses to these questions must perforce be laced with generous doses of caution, doubt and uncertainty.

NOTES

1. Japan, in William McCord's view (*The Dawn of the Pacific Century* [New Brunswick, N.J.: Transaction, 1993]), constitutes the "first tier" of Asian growth, with South Korea, Taiwan, Hong Kong and Singapore forming the second tier.

2. The operation and nurture of cartels in postwar Japan are detailed by Mark Tilton in *Restrained Trade* (Ithaca, N.Y.: Cornell University Press, 1996).

3. John Alic et al., *Beyond Spinoff* (Boston: Harvard Business School Press, 1992).

4. Chalmers Johnson has succinctly reviewed the diverse forms state activism has taken in Asia ("Comparative Capitalism: The Japanese Difference," *California Management Review* [Summer 1993]: 51–67).

5. See, for instance, Alasdair Bowie, "The Dynamics of Business-Government Relations in Industrializing Malaysia," in Andrew Macintyre (ed.), *Business and Government in Industrializing Asia* (Ithaca, N.Y.: Cornell University Press, 1994), pp. 167–94.

6. Paul Hutchcroft, "Booty Capitalism: Business-Government Relations in the Philippines," in Macintyre, *Business and Government in Industrializing Asia*, pp. 216–43.

7. Johnson, "Comparative Capitalism."

8. Jeffrey Hart provides an excellent comparison of the Japanese, American and European versions of capitalism in *Rival Capitalists* (Ithaca, N.Y.: Cornell University Press, 1992).

9. For an illuminating account of Motorola's efforts, backed by the U.S. government, to level Japan's playing fields and of other efforts by the state to coordinate American semiconductor firms' strategies, see Hedrick Smith, *Rethinking America* (New York: Random House, 1995).

10. Gerald Segal, *The Fate of Hong Kong* (New York: St. Martin's Press, 1993).

11. Kenichi Ohmae, *The Borderless World* (New York: HarperCollins, 1900); Kenichi Ohmae, *The End of the Nation State* (New York: Free Press, 1995).

12. Both revenues and expenditures as a percentage of GDP are far lower in Japan than in most Western economies at a comparable level of advancement, as Daniel Okimoto points out in *Between MITI and the Market* (Stanford, Calif.: Stanford University Press, 1989).

13. James Fallows' *Looking at the Sun* (New York: Pantheon, 1994) contrasts the route pursued by the twentieth century's dominant powers (Britain and the United States) with the statist mode adopted in Germany and Japan. He argues, with special reference to the semiconductor industry (presumably with generalizability to all technology-intensive industries), that strategic trade and technology can help create comparative advantage.

14. Trevor Matthews and John Ravenhill, "Strategic Trade Policy: The Northeast Asian Experience," in Macintyre, *Business and Government in Industrializing Asia*, pp. 42–46.

15. Ibid., pp. 46–56.

16. For fascinating insights into the multiple "access" points to Japanese firms available to MITI and the use of intermediate, industry-wide organizations by MITI, see Okimoto's *Between MITI and the Market*, pp. 149–57.

17. Smith, *Rethinking America*.

18. Ibid., pp. 378–402.

19. Tilton, *Restrained Trade*, p. 15.

20. See, for instance, Kiyoshi Suzaki, *The New Manufacturing Challenge* (New York: Free Press, 1987).

21. Michael Lind, "The Catalytic State," *The National Interest* (Spring 1992): 3–12.

22. Smith, *Rethinking America*, pp. 317–44.

23. The overall integrity of the military governments' efforts to achieve "condensed" growth is clearly documented in Cho Soon's *The Dynamics of Korean Economic Development* (Washington, D.C.: Institute for International Economics, 1994).

24. World Bank, *The East Asian Miracle* (New York: Oxford University Press, 1993), pp. 40–46.

25. Matthews and Ravenhill, "Strategic Trade Policy," pp. 58–66.

26. Ibid., pp. 66–70.

27. Ibid., p. 70.

28. Bowie, "The Dynamics of Business-Government Relations in Industrializing Malaysia," pp. 42–46.

29. Andrew Macintyre, "Power, Prosperity and Patrimonialism: Business and Government in Indonesia," in Macintyre, *Business and Government in Industrializing Asia*, pp. 244–67.

30. Ibid., pp. 254–58.

31. Anek Laothamatas, "From Clientelism to Partnership: Business-Government

Relations in Thailand," in Macintyre, *Business and Government in Industrializing Asia*, pp. 208–11.

32. Peter Waldman, the *Wall Street Journal*, October 4, 1996.

33. A fascinating, if horrifying, account of the excesses perpetrated during the cultural revolution is provided in Nicholas Kristof and Sheryl WuDunn, *China Wakes* (New York: Random House, 1994), pp. 70–79.

34. Jim Rohwer (*Asia Rising* [New York: Touchstone, 1995]) succinctly articulates the social obligations undertaken by the Chinese government for reasons as diverse as maintaining party control and attracting foreign investment, which, incidentally, may be intimately tied to each other (pp. 140–56).

35. "A Survey of India," *The Economist*, February 22, 1997, pp. 3–4.

36. Ibid., pp. 5–14.

3

The Nation-State Lives

Among the many issues debated in the United States, few have covered as much ground, occupied as much time or been as acrimonious as that over the nature, culture and future of the welfare system. Part of a larger debate—"battle" seems like a more appropriate word—over making government itself leaner and more effective, public opinion seems to be coalescing around the view that "welfare as we know it" is in urgent need of fine-tuning or, more likely, radical surgery. Starting from a premise that a capitalistic state must (1) acknowledge that a fraction of the population will not be able to fend for itself and (2) make provision in its budget for helping this relatively small segment, the U.S. government, starting in the 1930s, had, in a classic case of "policy creep," progressively taken on more responsibility to care for the have-nots in the country.[1] To many political and economic conservatives, the convergence of the social turmoil of the 1960s, feminist activism, preferential treatment of minorities, the need to be consistently and scrupulously politically correct and, in general, a pervasive sense that caring for the underdog and the disadvantaged, far from being unorthodox, are the new orthodoxy. It would appear, as a result, that, though the welfare system is not likely to be demolished, major changes are being proposed and implemented, signaling a limit to capitalism's humanity.[2] There have also been calls to terminate or at least moderate so-called corporate welfare, that is, subsidies and incentives given to firms to enable them to survive foreign competition or, in the case of foreign companies, to locate in the United States. However, based on the premise that corporations create jobs—even if it costs in the neighborhood of $200,000 per job, as was true of Mercedes Benz when it was lured to Alabama—while payments to single mothers and to unemployed and unemployable individuals discourage seeking work, it is extremely unlikely that government expenditures in this area will be curtailed. Indeed, given the clout that firms, particularly the larger, more internationally based ones, enjoy in Washington, it would be foolish to expect any action from either conservative or liberal ends of the political spectrum. Other compartments in the federal budget that appear too sacred to tinker with are education—in spite of occasional protests from advocates of greater private sector involvement—and defense. Citing the need to improve the quality of human resources to meet the skill and knowledge levels needed in coming decades, government expenditures on education are, in fact, likely to rise over the next decade.[3] Where defense is concerned, the end of the cold war has not as yet resulted in any significant "peace bonus." Standing at around one-fifth of the federal budget, military expenditures exceed outlays on education and health and rival the noncontributed (i.e., Social Security) portion of the social program. There is, however, little concerted opposition to these fairly large chunks of money being spent on defense. The realization that the dangers posed by the Soviet Empire have been replaced by other and quite different, perhaps even more alarming and unpredictable threats has no doubt contributed to the willingness to give the military a bigger piece of the pie than it might ostensibly be entitled to.

Asian governmental expenditures have, over the years spanning their greatest economic growth, been relatively far smaller and not directed toward areas emphasized in the United States or, for that matter, Western Europe. True, education has attracted a high level of government support, particularly at the primary level, and the adoption of such a focus has indubitably paid off. However, military budgets have typically been a fraction of their levels in Europe or America. This has been true even of Japan, South Korea and Taiwan, all three of which have, by any reckoning, had to deal with historical and/or ideological enmities over the half century since the Second World War. Though Japan and, to a lesser extent, Taiwan and South Korea have sharply increased their defense spending to assume an increasingly fair share of the cost of protecting themselves, the proportion of their budgets devoted to defense still falls far short of the outlays of their Western allies. In passing, an irony comes to mind: the economic protectionism practiced by these and other Asian countries served to defend themselves from their *allies*, while most of them did but little to protect themselves from their implacable political adversaries. Equally ironic is the distaste shown by certain Asian countries (Malaysia) for Western values, both cultural and political, when their survival and present success, in large part, are attributable to the very values they now criticize so stridently.

While we look at the entire picture framed within the term "Asian values" in Chapter 6, it is also germane to our present discussion to evaluate the impact of Asian cultures on government policy. (I say "cultures" since there is no distinct Asian culture; in fact, multiple cultures exist within most nations within the region.) True, given the strength of family bonds on the continent, the need for the government to come to the rescue of the less fortunate is minimized, in comparison to the United States and Europe. There might be parts of Europe (e.g., southern Italy) where the family support system is still strong, but, on the whole, most people in mature industrial nations have had to become more task-oriented, mobile, impersonal and, in general, governed by the financial needs of the ubiquitous large organization.

How, then, have East Asian and Southeast Asian countries managed to remain immune from "industrial diseases" like crime, loneliness and deprivation? Have they found or devised a magic charm that wards off the evils associated with rapid growth? As we see later in this book, they have not quite managed to avoid the maladies of success and plenty. Not even Singapore and Malaysia, notwithstanding the former's compact size, the latter's Islamic society and both nations' seemingly unending stream of homilies on Asian values, have been unaffected by the ingress of foreign technologies and ideologies. There are, however, factors that have helped moderate the rate of societal change, acting perhaps to both slow down and delay its response to economic progress. The Chinese family-based business network is one such factor.[4] The Chinese diaspora in countries as diverse as Taiwan, Malaysia, Thailand, Hong Kong, Singapore and the Philippines has tended to form business alliances based on family, village and other bonds both within and across countries, resulting in families and the kinship-bond networks assuming responsibility for education, old age care, emergency needs and so on. In countries where the governments are not favorably disposed to the Chinese minority (say, Malaysia and, to a lesser extent, Indonesia) social self-responsibility undoubtedly is essential, while in other states (e.g., Taiwan, Singapore) where traditional Confucian values prevail, governments need spend no more than minimally on social causes. Though countries in the developed world also started on the path to industrialization backed by strong family units, which started crumbling in the face of the pressures that modern society and its organizations exert, the Chinese family is likely to withstand a similar debilitation more effectively, or at least for a longer period of time. The centrality of ancestor worship and filial piety to these cultures makes the family integral to the survival not just of the belief system but of the business system as well. Of course, as the exigencies of global competition, less benign government policies and the need to find new markets confront them, Chinese family businesses will become increasingly permeated by outside influences. The family's influence and, indeed, its integrity also could well be gradually shaken in the years to come. The other nations in the region, whether Confucian (e.g., Korea, Japan), Islamic (Malaysia and Indonesia), Buddhist (Thailand), Christian (Philippines, Korea) or Hindu (India), also have strong family loyalties, suggesting that government outlays on social ends could continue at low levels, making for a much smaller governmental role in the lives of its citizens.[5] However, the jury is still out on whether or how long Asia can avert the onset of growth-related social problems.

Japan appears to be an obvious refutation of the thesis that industrialization inevitably requires the government to play a bigger role in society, particularly in areas that would not attract private investment. Social services have not grown appreciably in the Japanese budget over the past 20 years. Old age pensions and health care for the elderly are part of corporate budgets, while education has always been a government responsibility and has not, therefore, been a new line item on the budget. The impression that Japan's government is, as so often claimed, minimalist in terms of expenditures is, however, quickly dispelled when one observes the operation of the "civil minimum," as Kenichi Ohmae terms it, in Japan.[6] The civil minimum, a phenomenon certainly not unknown in other developed countries, is the provision of specific—and often an expanding range of—services to all segments of the population and areas of the country regardless of the cost to the exchequer and, ultimately, to the taxpayer. Roads, railway lines, telephone connections and other public utilities are, of course, part of most countries' civil minimum and are typically not questioned wherever they are implemented. Electricity lines are strung, for instance, to new homes that are within reasonable distance of existing connections, the cost being recovered by suitably adjusting the utility's tariff. However, as Ohmae points out, the circumstances are unique in Japan. Rice farmers, who constitute a fraction of 1% of the population (even when one counts the part-time farmers, they amount to no more than 3% of the Japanese) and whose inefficiency is rewarded with large subsidies, are resented by the rest of the population. The resentment intensifies when working persons in Tokyo or Osaka reflect that their taxes help keep their rural fellow citizens afloat, while they themselves suffer through long commutes, live in cramped apartments and pay grossly inflated prices for food. Their thoughts turn increasingly bitter when they see—on television or on one of their trips abroad, trips that are among the few palliatives in their state of wealthy deprivation—how their counterparts in the Western world, especially the United States, live. Hasn't Japan outsmarted the rest of the world with its excellence in quality, manufacturing, marketing and other areas of management? Is this the same Japan, the salaryman ponders, whose governmental and corporate strategies have struck terror in the hearts of all who had the misfortune to cross swords with them? Can this, in fact, be the much-vaunted Japan, Inc.—no more than a mere peddler of pork? Indeed, says Ohmae, it is. Not only is Japanese agricultural productivity woefully low, but it consumes land that would ease the housing shortage and make the resource available to the highly productive secondary and tertiary sectors. The overwhelming bulk of Japan's wealth is created in the Tokyo, Osaka and Nagoya prefectures, the other 44 prefectures serving as recipients of largesse. Small towns and cities numbering in the thousands have generous budgets financed by Tokyo, with which they have undertaken construction programs, often on a grand scale. Bridges, libraries, indoor stadia, concert halls, dams and barriers are constructed at considerable expense, often unnecessarily.

Contributions from the hundreds of thousands of construction companies are crucial to ensuring that the political status quo is maintained. Bureaucrats who administer the various subsidy and expenditure programs also have a vested interest in their continued existence. Japan should not be singled out for its persistence in domestic profligacy both to keep foreign products out and to lend a helping hand to local firms and job seekers. Korea, Taiwan, Malaysia, Thailand and the rest have no less active governments when it comes to spending money at home. The creaking infrastructure in all of Asia is expected to soak up around $1 trillion over the next decade, and local companies could reap a bonanza.[7] Whether to build or rebuild highways, improve communications, or clean up environmental messes created by unfettered industrial growth or the shifting of a capital city (as Malaysia is in the process of doing, from Kuala Lumpur to Putrajaya), the need for governments to invest heavily in the interest of society as a whole, but even more so to the benefit of the contract-winning corporations—some of which have close links with the politicians and parties in power—is not likely to diminish in the foreseeable future. For governments that have excelled in reaping the rewards of Keynesian, rather than Schumpeterian, efficiency[8] (i.e., with the state, not technological and managerial innovation, as drivers of the economy), these additional government expenditures, particularly for nations as well heeled as most in the region now are, are not likely to break the bank. (The less wealthy nations like China and India whose tax revenues cannot support the levels of capital needed for infrastructural development are offering build-operate-transfer contracts to foreign firms so as to ease the present pain somewhat.) The point, however, is that old habits die hard. Governments that have a history of guidance, intervention and "persuasion" of firms and individuals to pursue policies they deem appropriate are likely to continue behaving in similar fashion even when conditions no longer appear to warrant it. Far from being "catalytic" (a notion refuted earlier), they become "addicted" states. Intervention becomes a tradition, a part of the political and bureaucratic culture. Korea, for instance, whose *chaebol* are aggressively pursuing automobile markets all over the world—particularly in the European Community, India and China—still has tariffs making auto imports prohibitively costly, distribution channels are difficult to gain entry into, while setting up manufacturing facilities can hardly be described as a straightforward process. Korea is obviously "doing a Japan," though the 1% share that foreign auto firms have labored to achieve is even less than that in the mother of all protective nations, Japan. Even a state as ostensibly open to foreign investment as Malaysia—in part, to end the dominance of the Chinese minority, as noted earlier—and with a stated preference for private investment has, both in its large infrastructural projects and in privatization efforts, revealed a strong, all-too-visible hand of the government. Favors granted to supporters of the ruling party and contracts awarded to firms run by the party have resulted in a windfall for the politicians governing the country.[9] Far from distancing the state from the market, these actions have created a proxy for the state, creating the illusion of a disinterested, uninvolved government. Addicts are notorious for not admitting to their craving, and, in fact, the denial may ring true to themselves, so wrapped up are they in their own pattern of behavior. Governments with a long history of tinkering with, and manipulating, the operation of markets while disclaiming any ability, desire or need to do so are unlikely to desist from their labors once they are well on their way to accomplishing their mission (as in the case of Thailand and Malaysia) or have, in fact, done so (e.g., Japan and perhaps South Korea). The addicted state, adhering to the maxim "If it ain't broke, don't fix it," continues on its merry way, oblivious to the fact that its past achievements rested upon conditions that no longer exist. All the Asian nations that have emerged from the shadows of poverty have done so through concerted export drives, curbing of imports unless for technology enhancement, using a combination of the carrot and the stick to point organizations in the "right" direction and letting it be known that protection would not last forever. The reality, however, has turned out to be that, as growth occurred, it came packaged with other kinds of problems. Whether these problems directly resulted from government policies or were autonomous in origin is immaterial. States have felt compelled to act in defense of their national well-being and honor. Urging Japanese to take foreign trips in order to reduce the surplus and thus deflect U.S. attention away from them, while at the same time dragging their feet over improving market access in industries like photography and paper, inducing Thais to save more, Chinese orders clamping down on use of the Internet for communicating political news, India's halting progress in approving foreign investment in power projects and South Korea's directive to a telecom company to limit its imports (in this instance, from the United States) are some of the signs of addicted states' inability to disengage themselves from the process of growth and development once it is well under way.

Another possible explanation for the phenomenon's persistence apart from the ones already cited (the state's belief in its own efficacy and a desire to continue wielding authority or, more succinctly, the culture and politics of intervention) is that most countries in the region have been governed by a person or a cohesive coterie over the period under study. South Korea, for much of its phase of rapid growth, was governed either by military men who brooked no opposition or by authoritarian civilians equally ruthless in their actions. Generals Park and Chun, for instance, governed during periods of heady growth and saw themselves (and their iron rule) as the saviors of the Korean nation. Their desire to build organizations capable of taking on the world led to the rise of the *chaebol*, the provision of credit to them on easy terms, their insulation from foreign competition at home and so on. The flaws that have become apparent subsequently in this policy—for example, the duplication of product lines among the conglomerates, the poor investment of easy money—may have contributed, in part, to the faltering of the Korean "miracle." The civilian government that took over from General Chun has persisted with similar policies, resulting in even more maladies besetting the Korean economy, compounded by the inability to put a lid on labor unrest. Democratic reforms are *not* the source of Korea's problems, however. They are merely a convenient scapegoat. The desire to continue with what worked in the past, long after such actions have outlived their usefulness, is the main cause of the Korean state's discomfiture. Of course, revelations of corruption and the dispensation of favors only serve to further tarnish a policy framework, which, at the appropriate time, was beneficial to the national purpose.

No discussion of favoritism, cronyism and nepotism over the past 20 years would be complete without mention of President Suharto and Indonesia.[10] Taking over from a megalomaniac (Sukarno) in a country where socialism had been enshrined as the philosophy of governance and a society in which violence against the Chinese minority was a normal occurrence—arising perhaps from resentment of their success in business during the Dutch rule as well as after independence—Suharto has essentially, since assuming power, ridden to glory on Chinese shoulders by treating them preferentially in the awarding of contracts and in approvals of investment proposals. As the Chinese networks based in East and Southeast Asia began to prosper and flex their muscles, trusting the power of the Chinese makes even more sense—tycoons like Liem Sioe Liong heading powerful Indonesian conglomerates not only have access to the war chests they have accumulated over years of patiently cultivating relationships with the government (i.e., President Suharto and his kith and kin) but can draw upon the expertise and billions commanded by Robert Kuok in Malaysia, Gordon Woo in Hong Kong or any of the numerous multimillionaires in the Chinese network in Asia. Why, then, should Suharto deviate from a policy that has seen his country achieve 7 to 8% rates of growth over more than a decade and helped to enrich him and his near and dear, even if it makes the country beholden to a disliked minority or to foreign companies that are willing to play the mutually beneficial back-scratching game? Malaysia's Mahathir Mohammed has been in office for not nearly quite so long as Suharto, but his writ runs as large in his country as Suharto's does in the archipelago nation. Mahathir is, by no stretch of the imagination, as strong a "family man" (irony intended) as Suharto, but his durability has served to convince him that his actions and philosophies are just what the doctor ordered for his country. Who can argue with success? Or with a leader who, following in the hallowed tradition of other Asian leaders notoriously impatient with dissent, stifles all opposition to his rule by equating himself to his country?[11] Taiwan has had its share of authoritarianism under the aegis of the Kuomintang (KMT), while Japan, certainly no dictatorship over the past half century, has been governed almost uninterruptedly by the Liberal Democratic Party (LDP). The Japanese government has been headed by a series of faceless leaders who have faithfully carried out the will of the party to ensure its continued survival and success. (They exemplify the willingness common to many species in nature to sacrifice the individual and the present in the interest of the group and the future.) China's communists might appear to break the mold—there was a marked discontinuity in government policy in 1979, when the economy was opened and freed up. However, the government's desire to maintain control over the extent and nature of foreign investment, the gradual expansion of special economic zones, sensitivity to information dissemination and so on clearly signal its intent to direct the economy and, indeed, the country on a predetermined path. How far it will succeed in this purpose is not so much a function of the state's will—which is indomitable—and its resources—which are extensive—but of the unpredictable nature of forces that could be unleashed in a market economy, *permitted* to function because it serves the purposes of the authoritarian state.[12] India's government, in contrast to that of China, has little that is authoritarian about it—more's the pity, in view of many Indians. India's democracy, as is true of most democracies, accommodates a diversity of interests and needs, often resulting in much populist rhetoric and little action. Ruled by the Congress Party for most of the postindependence (1947) period, the policies have tended to be socialistic, with the government as protector of the common good and spender of first resort. Private firms have existed and prospered either on sufferance or on the basis of family contacts with government leaders. The tradition of paternal relations between the state, on one hand, and the people and business, on the other, has apparently persisted even after economic reforms were instituted in 1991. Political parties gain electorally by denigrating the slow pace of change and the unfeeling character of the free market, by adopting budget-busting social programs and by issuing xenophobic diatribes against rapacious multinationals. While the Indian people are not as accustomed to the guarantees (jobs, health care etc.) provided in erstwhile communist states like East Germany, the fear of trading a known, albeit ineffective, system for one whose potential for damage has been luridly expanded upon by self-seeking politicians is, to many, a frightening prospect indeed.[13]

If the developmental state has given way to the addicted state with politicians, bureaucrats, corporations and the public-at-large converging to defend national economic gains, policies and goals oriented toward the achievement of their ends might appear to be solidly entrenched. Economic nationalism, whether it is based on domestic or foreign capital and technology, is not an immovable object, however. Even if it has seemed to be a power unto itself in the past, the nation-state is being buffeted by the forces of globalization. Factories established in Malaysia, Singapore, Thailand or Indonesia to take advantage of low labor rates and other attractive features (often provided by the government) can just as easily be shifted to other locations offering even more.[14] When low labor rates are combined with generous government policies *and* a growing, perhaps affluent potential customer base (as in the case of China and, more gradually, India), MNEs are not likely to hesitate. Just as they demonstrated little loyalty to their home countries in relocating to their adopted homes, they are not likely to feel, or even be capable of feeling, any sympathy for the countries they are now abandoning in pursuit of their all-too-material dreams. When one considers that nearly 40% of all world trade comprises intrafirm exchanges, the potential for massive shifts, as countries climb the ladder of development, is likely to intensify.[15] Today, China, the Philippines and perhaps India are the favored locations. Tomorrow it could well be Mozambique or Peru. Do nations have any say in what MNEs do anymore? Or are they increasingly going to be cast in the invidious role of supplicants, dependent on the largesse of peripatetic enterprises? Kenichi Ohmae argues that the nation-state's days are numbered.[16] In his view nationhood is a concept that has outlived its usefulness. For instance, northern Italy has more in common with Germany and England than it does with the southern portion of Italy, which, in turn, has a greater affinity to Spain and Portugal. This appears to be in line with Huntington's thesis that the great unifying (and, hence, dividing) force of the next few decades will be culture. Nation-states formed by force-fitting diverse cultures into their confines are, in this interpretation, likely to fracture along the same lines into their cultural molecules, so to speak. Barber's contention that "jihad," that is, ancient cultural, religious and allied animosities, is sprouting and will continue to proliferate in the years ahead suggests a similar atomistic tendency in the world of the late twentieth century.[17] Barber tempers his prognostications of our fissile future by positing that global corporations, particularly the ones in the vanguard of the cultural export revolution, despite the various blandishments they offer to the unwary, help bring the world together. McDonald's, Coke, Levis, Marlboro and the other so-called global brands, along with Western, particularly American, television and film, (all of which, acting in concert, comprise the forces of McWorld), create a demand for a lifestyle and a convergence toward behavior patterns that acts as a counterfoil to the divisive forces of jihad.[18] Jihad and McWorld are antagonistic to each other in other ways, too. For instance, the tradition-bound, root-seeking behavior urged in the one is opposed by the materialism and outward orientation of the other. While rock-throwing Palestinians and club-wielding Hindu fundamentalists might appear to be compromising their principles by wearing Nikes and using Kodak film, they will tell you that these artifacts are no more than conveniences, that, given control over their destinies, they will put the powerful multinationals in their place. Just as surely as "cultural globalism" provides an integrating influence balancing the separateness born of a sense of historic differences, the two, under the appropriate conditions, could also work in tandem. The forces of fusion—both the cultural bonds generated by brand images and the traditional convergence momentum created by a widely shared desire to improve one's economic lot—are typically transnational in nature, bringing together countries or parts of countries that have reached similar levels of development.[19] Ohmae, for example, makes the point that countries whose per capita income exceeds $5,000 differ markedly from those below this line of demarcation. The types of goods demanded—automobiles, computers, insurance, appliances—change as a country makes this income transition. Thailand and Malaysia, therefore, bear greater market similarities to each other and to say, South Korea than they do to neighboring Myanmar (better known as Burma before it reverted to its precolonial name).[20] The blurring of differences among nations as they develop industrially is, of course, not a new phenomenon. The fact that the behavior of consumers in Hong Kong bears a greater resemblance to that in London than to the tastes of Chinese consumers and that cities across the world bear a greater resemblance to one another than to rural areas within their respective nations has been remarked upon and discussed before. There is, however, a slight—or perhaps not quite so slight—difference today. Among countries developing along parallel paths, the transnational sense of community does little to bridge the rifts that might exist within them. Just because the Israeli and the Palestinian, the Irish and the English, the Hindu and the Muslim and the Uighur and the Han (perhaps even the lion and the lamb?) appear to be coming together in the pursuit of wealth and the desire to participate in building an economic civilization, the conclusion that they will coexist peacefully does not necessarily follow. In fact, the accelerating pace of economic growth and consumer commonalities might exacerbate the tendency toward separateness, if not disintegration. Income disparities within countries could, for instance, create simmering resentments, pitting the haves against have-nots, the city versus the village and ruler against ruled. The World Bank contends that income disparities in East and Southeast Asia have, on the whole, been remarkably low.[21] The Gini coefficient (a comparison of the top and bottom 20% of incomes) indicates that even Indonesia, all anecdotal incidence to the contrary, is a relatively egalitarian society. Of course, the World Bank, in its haste to justify the so-called free market policy regimen adopted in much of the region (a regimen that, we have seen, was, and is, by no means government-free), does not say anything about the cronyism rampant in Indonesia or the fact that the ratio of incomes of the top 1% to those of the bottom 20% would not appear to be quite so flattering. (Reason: the top 1% earn much more than those just below them on the economic ladder, and the earnings of the latter tend to depress the average income of the elite and, with it, the disparity index.) Income disparities, though not as endemic or vast as in, say, parts of Latin America or Africa, nevertheless exist in much of Asia and are, in addition to cultural and ethnic differences, a fertile breeding ground for the divisive forces collectively labeled jihad. The concentration of wealth in Kuala Lumpur relative to the rest of Malaysia, the lopsided economic power of Bangkok in an otherwise underdeveloped Thailand and the dominant role played by Guangdong and Shenzen in China's rise provide clear evidence of the localization of growth in the story of Asia's development. The income ratio (upward of five to one) between the SEZs and the rest of China has been responsible, in part, for a huge transient population—anywhere up to 200 million people—in search of the El Dorado of highly paid, guaranteed jobs.[22]

Growth triangles further compound the centrifugal forces at work in societies breaking out of the clasp of poverty. Conceived and created to make full use of the capabilities and resources offered by an alliance among different regions (often in different countries), growth triangles are especially popular in East and Southeast Asia. The Guangdong—Hong Kong–Taiwan growth triangle—stands out as an example of complementary collaboration that helps sustain development.[23] While the mainland location of Guangdong provides the low wage and, in general, low factor cost, Hong Kong functions as a source of capital, while Taiwan's technology enables production of exportable goods. Though the exports are mainly to developed countries, maintaining a pattern that has brought considerable success to all the involved countries over the years, the tripartite symbiosis calls for intra-Asian technology transfer and trade, reducing somewhat the dependence on foreign MNEs. Of course, the fact that some of the transfers occurring do so between sovereign countries should not be forgotten; that is, though Taipei is frequently referred to, particularly by those who wish to mollify the mainland Chinese, as Taipei, China, the nation known as Taiwan is no figment of the imagination. If the political party in power in Taiwan decided that it did not wish to share expertise in computers or biotechnology with its giant neighbor, the growth triangle could well find itself lacking a technological sponsor. If the unthinkable happens, and a flight of capital were to occur away from Hong Kong, bankrolling the investment on the mainland might become far more sticky. Just because ethnic similarities exist, and people feel a sense of shared identity, the indefinite continuance of what is presently an economically beneficial arrangement cannot be taken for granted. As the levels of income, technology and expectations grow in that vertex of the triangle that started from the lowest levels in all three of these dimensions (Guangdong/Fujian in the PRC in this instance), the rapidly developing vertex is likely to demand more in the form of economic returns, to increasingly flex its muscles and to begin striking out on its own. The Singapore–Johore (Malaysia)–Riau (Indonesia) growth triangle, whose "lead vertex" is Singapore,[24] has been established to take advantage of complementarities paralleling those in the southern China instance mentioned earlier and is also subject to the same future uncertainties. Indeed, when Singapore's former prime minister Lee Kuan Yew (now given the modest title of senior minister to make clear his emeritus status) made insulting references to the quality of life in Johore Bahru, he was roundly excoriated in the Malaysian press and taken to task by prominent politicians in that country. Apparently, while each partner in the triangle has much to gain from the others and has cultivated transnational ties, national psyches are still as tender, and egos as easily bruised as before.[25] Ironically, Lee is the original engineer on the Asian values train. His criticism of a fellow Asian nation, of which his city-state was once part, and the fallout that resulted drive home the point that much more than economic complementarity and cultural similarity is needed for growth triangles to be a lasting success. This is even truer when the transnational venture involves more than three countries that are widely disparate in politics, factor conditions, culture and ethnicity. The Tumen River Delta economic zone is an example of this sort of ambitious undertaking, encompassing, as it does, parts of northern China, South and North Korea, Mongolia, eastern Russia and Japan. The potential obviously is enormous, but so is the likelihood that self-interest and the dynamics inherent to any situation of catch-up (e.g., higher wage rates, improved technological capabilities) could combine to make membership less attractive to some of the constituents as time goes by.

   In addition to the transient nationalism of globalization and the transnationalism of regional alliances such as growth triangles and economic zones, the nation-state's viability is further threatened by the emergence of extranationalism. The perception that certain nations have convergent interests, the conviction that an association of contiguous nations must cooperate for their mutual benefit and perhaps the desire to exclude outsiders from gaining at the expense of the consortium have contributed to the creation (spawning might be a better word) of numerous collections of nations. The European Community (EC), the North American Free Trade Agreement (NAFTA), the Association of Southeast Asian Nations (ASEAN), Asia Pacific Economic Cooperation (APEC), and South Asian Association for Regional Cooperation (SAARC) are some of the well-known and not so well known national groupings functioning or attempting to function in various parts of the world. The EC has perhaps come closest to unifying diverse countries in a common cause—their individual and collective good. Though many hurdles remain to be cleared—an agreement on a common currency, for instance, prickly issues such as possible domination by Germany and a decision of how many more countries should be admitted—the EC is, at the very least, a purposeful coalition, not a motley collection of nation-states, each pursuing its own agenda. True, national identities die hard; the French are not likely to change their lifestyles or eschew their Gallic pride in their art and history, the British are not eager to accept the German mark as the coinage of the realm and the Italians are not likely to allow one of their giant firms (e.g., Fiat) to voluntarily downsize just because Volkswagen in Germany or Nissan in England makes cars more efficiently. Even more trouble could ensue in deciding which other countries to admit to the club (which will no longer remain as exclusive as it now seems) and in the potential for conflict that exists with an enlarged, more diverse membership. Should Turkey, Hungary and Poland be admitted? How would Turkey's admission affect the policies enacted in Germany regarding "guest workers," many of whom are of Turkish origin? If the former Council for Mutual Economic Assistance (COMECON) countries need a helping hand with their economies, will the rest of the EC reach out to them? As the nations of Europe dance— carefully—with each other, each stepping to the native tunes it so cherishes, jostling each other on an increasingly crowded floor, an air of bonhomie may not always prevail. The EC, undoubtedly, is the articulation of that most human of all drives: self-preservation. The threats posed by the rest of a predatory world, initially the United States, the communist world, and Japan, but of late encompassing much of Asia, to defenseless "loners," not the desire to rise above petty national interests and squabbles, underlie the birth and subsequent evolution of the EC. Nevertheless, to reiterate, it is perhaps the most successful experiment yet conducted, without the use of force, in uniting sovereign states in a common economic and political mission. Other alliances are far looser in both structure and operations. NAFTA, for instance, operates more like a mammoth growth triangle in that it attempts to combine the complementary aspects of three diverse countries—Mexico, with a population as large as Germany's but the majority of whom are poor; Canada, sparsely populated yet rich in output and resources; the United States, with the world's largest economy and very prickly about its independence, job preservation and immigration, illegal or otherwise. The United States dominates NAFTA as no country, not even Germany, dominates the EC. Yet, the concerns in the United States over the effect NAFTA has had on American employment, "sucking" away manufacturing jobs and leaving no more than a shell of a production base behind, are far more intense and insistent. The U.S. situation is analogous to Germany's if both Britain and France were low factor cost locations and were inviting German firms to move to either attractive location from which they then proceeded to export to Germany at the preferential rate applicable to community members. As things stand, most countries in Europe have enacted local content laws aimed at keeping out "unfair" competition, especially from countries with low wages and/or superior production/deisgn technology. With large supply centers for exportable products in their midst, EC members might well have scaled heights of paranoia they have not exhibited so far. The admission of countries like Turkey, Hungary and possibly other countries in Eastern Europe could escalate fears and activism on both the right and the left. Neither of these extremes—or, for that matter, many in the mainstream—lacks the motivation and energy to press home its allergy to extranational linkages and dependencies. ASEAN, unlike both the EC and NAFTA, was started to monitor common political and military interests.[26] It was initially used as a forum to help formulate mutually beneficial policies and resolve disparities. In fact, when the Chinese with their newfound confidence, bordering on cockiness as the power to reckon with in Asia, occupied a Vietnamese island in the Paracel group, the ASEAN membership were vocal in their support for their beleaguered comrade, just as they had made common cause with the Philippines when the Chinese decided that they needed more of the Spratly Islands. For all its combined economic clout, though, the ASEAN finds itself in the same invidious position as a herd of zebras being pursued by a starving lion. The herd feels great empathy for the victim selected by the predator but is extremely unlikely to collectively come to the rescue—an action that, in all likelihood will help their fellow zebra escape—by ignoring, for the moment, the instinct for survival and the consciousness of their particular identity. If, for instance, the members of ASEAN were to consider themselves to be part of a whole greater than the individual entities constituting it, they would be a formidable foe or ally, depending on the circumstances. However, despite the fact that they are an economically powerful grouping, their unwillingness to rise above their sense of identity as individual nation-states is a significant chink in their armor. Moreover, even in the economic sense, ASEAN does not present a unified face to the rest of the world. Dependent as the region has been on exports to industrialized nations and on investment flowing in from Japan, the United States and Taiwan, as these factors weaken—that is, the demand for its goods is not increasing rapidly, if at all, in the developed nations, more countries are jumping on the export bandwagon and foreign capital has more options to choose from—country is pitted against country in the race to stay ahead. Export markets and capital availability are both becoming zero-sum games.

Even less viable than ASEAN as a collaborative device or conflict resolution mechanism is APEC.[27] Consisting of nations as diverse as the United States, Chile, Japan, China and the Philippines, the most that APEC can hope to achieve is the awareness that all its members border the Pacific Ocean and, therefore, have the opportunity to do business with one another. APEC unquestionably provides a showcase for each country's leaders to be seen with his or her counterparts from member countries. If ceremony helped import restrictions, and cordiality led to the transfer of technology, configurations such as APEC would be unqualified successes. A recent APEC meeting, while providing a useful forum for publicity—leaders anxious to be seen playing the roles of international statesmen and stateswomen—did not even broach potentially contentious issues such as lowering barriers to the entry of foreign service (e.g., insurance) providers. Strangely enough, even an agglomeration as nebulous as APEC or one as powerless as ASEAN is seen to be advantageous to its constituents. Membership, in the words of a credit card company's slogan, has its privileges— or so exclusion from clubs like the EC, APEC and ASEAN makes clear. India, for instance, would dearly love to achieve even associate status in ASEAN and be considered for APEC membership. Being a latecomer to the government-sponsored free market bash, India would like to gain access to some of the preferential trading privileges accorded by membership in these associations. Of course, once its catch-up effort gains momentum, the charms of belonging to mutually beneficial groups will fade. But until that occurs, countries like India will need a herd of their own. SAARC,[28] which is essentially a political association established much like ASEAN to address issues of mutual political significance, does not appear capable of assuming an economic role as well. Though its members signed a Preferential Trading Agreement establishing lower tariffs for intraregional trade, the success of this bloc, as with any other, does not depend solely on economic considerations. Cultural, political and religious animosities need to be put aside, and the group's largest partners must make concessions to allay fears of the least powerful countries. There have been preliminary discussions on forming an Indian Ocean trading zone in which India and South Africa would be the dominant members. The geographic spread and vast diversity of membership make this a doubtful starter, the strongest motivating force being pique at being left out of the action.

Apart from regional or extranational groupings that seem to exert pressure on the nation-state to conform to the needs of the collective, certain supranational bodies also call for the same acquiescence in serving the common good. The World Bank, GATT and its successor, the grandiosely named World Trade Organization (WTO), all strive to achieve broad acceptance of certain policy regimens and norms of international trade.[29] The World Bank typically has no mandate to enforce its will or prescriptions on any country—unless the bank's financial resources are needed to bail a troubled economy out of its economic woes. In the event of being requested to rescue a floundering economy (Mexico, India and Argentina being some of the many countries that found themselves in this situation), the World Bank can, and does, insist that its menu for recovery (such as reducing the deficit by curtailing government expenditures, relaxing controls on business, ensuring macroeconomic stability and so on) be scrupulously followed. The World Bank's role in most of Asia's government-led economic growth is no more than minimal, which means that little national autonomy has been sacrificed by most Asian countries in getting where they are now. The World Bank's obviously self-serving claims notwithstanding, East Asia's rise was based—as we have seen earlier—on a mix of free markets, import substitution, protectionism and industrial policy. GATT, unlike the World Bank, is not an agency that can help pull a country's chestnuts out of the fire. Its only purpose is to move the world toward a free trade regimen, eliminating all forms of quotas, tariffs and discriminatory trade protocols. GATT would prefer to see quotas give way to tariffs, the latter to be erased completely in the long run. Enforcement was beyond GATT's scope. The most it was capable of was to recommend that disputes be resolved consensually, failing which a decision would be handed down by an arbitrator. This decision, however, was nonbinding, which naturally meant that GATT held few terrors for countries intent on pursuing their self-interest in blithe disregard of GATT's philosophy of fair play and mutual accommodation. Covert protectionism, such as Japan's almost touching dedication to its antiquated distribution system which slams the door on newcomers (i.e., foreign interlopers), Korea's reluctance to allow its *chaebol* to be challenged at home and France's draconian local content laws have held firm in spite of GATT's strictures. The WTO may be viewed as GATT with teeth. The WTO can impose sanctions on countries not complying with its stipulations.[30] However, though GATT ruled against the EC for imposing stiff tariffs on agricultural imports, not much has happened under the aegis of the WTO to enforce the ruling. Agriculture, textiles and services are the most contentious areas. Farmers are notoriously resistant to competing against foreign producers on the basis of agricultural efficiency, textile production is a stepping-stone to higher value-added goods, though imports reduce employment in the developed world, and services from abroad are perceived as the new multinational threat to the independence of emerging nations like India and Brazil. The WTO, not unlike the United Nations (UN), will be most decisive and forceful in dealing with the weak and the friendless. Large trading economies, militarily strong nations, developing countries with burgeoning markets or significant investment from abroad and states adopting restrictive practices of which it is nearly impossible to adduce hard evidence are not likely to be singled out for punitive sanctions. In other words, the WTO's sword of righteousness is likely to remain sheathed or, even when drawn, swish harmlessly through the air, avoiding or missing its nimble rivals, who have seen this kind of feinting and parrying before. Asian countries, being past masters at the art of "agree and forget," have, and will continue to have, little difficulty with any limitations placed on their behavior by the WTO or any other supranational body. The pattern of resistance, giving way to reluctant agreement, and followed by a calculated disregard for the undertaking provided earlier and a set of well-reasoned excuses for noncompliance, constitutes the package of dissembling and, to use politically correct language, measured disregard for the truth that one can expect. Anyone who imagines that Malaysia, Thailand, China, South Korea, India, Indonesia or any of the other countries in Asia that have set their sights firmly on gaining ground on the West, will instead make and act upon concessions that will retard their rate of progress must indeed be naive. Of course, näiveté is far from being a rare characteristic among Western diplomats, policymakers and businesspeople. The pinnacle of credulity is scaled when the decision makers who matter share the opinion that keeping the lines of communication open and making concessions on trade, human rights and international law are likely to make the Chinese leadership join the comity of nations. This sort of ingenuousness would, indeed, be engaging (pun intended) if it were not based on such flimsy grounds. So long as the short-term needs of multinational corporations, of politicians eager to strike statesmanlike postures and of today's consumers are viewed as outweighing the rights of labor in developing nations, the *discipline* of trade, the needs of tomorrow's consumers everywhere and a concern for justice, organizations that claim to unite the world under their umbrella will be continuously subject to the pulling and hauling we term politics. Politics, as everyone knows, is all about the use of power. Power flows, certainly, from the barrel of a gun, but it also accrues to countries holding technological trump cards, vast or potentially vast markets and generous factor endowments, including low-cost labor and supplies of raw material.

A country may be part of a growth triangle or development zone, belong to a trade alliance of nations, be a member of the WTO or some/all of these groupings. However, whether or not it is a part of transnational, extranational or supranational (or all of them) associations, the unit of analysis or the entity in the thick of the action is the nation-state. While its economic function may well be to orchestrate the action without becoming a part of the fray, it must always be remembered that the nation-state, which has been the driving force behind the surge in prosperity in Asia since the 1970s, is essentially a political creature with political goals. The means used have been economic—in terms of fiscal, monetary and industrial policies—but the ultimate goals are political. Governments in Asia have, no doubt, consistently adopted policies aimed at lifting gross national product (GNP), incomes, technological capabilities, educational levels and so on. But the underlying purpose has always been to enhance the standing of the nation concerned relative to its neighbors and, more important, to the advanced countries of Europe and North America. Movement upward on the ladder of development has enabled countries like Japan, South Korea, Taiwan, Singapore, Malaysia and China to progressively become more self-confident and aggressive. Yes, nations are like people, because their leaders' attitudes and behaviors represent those of the countries they lead. I am not anthropomorphizing when I state that Singapore, Malaysia and China have become far more strident in proclaiming their virtues to the world after their stellar economic performance in the 1980s. Ideological purity is no longer a badge of honor, except perhaps in the circles frequented by Cuba's Castro. When people are prosperous, the ideology propounded by their leaders is given serious consideration. Apart from the prime goal of reputation enhancement, governments also avidly seek credit and praise for the country's rise, which could ensure the continued existence of these systems of government and of the group exercising power. All over Asia, governments have pursued their political goals through economic strategies, making it highly unlikely that the political mission of the nation-state will disappear as the economic strategies succeed. Just because a country enters into interdependent or regional relationships, we cannot conclude that it is sacrificing its sense of nationhood on the altar of economic advancement. Governments, particularly the addicted states we find in abundance in Asia, will continue to make the important economic decisions to guide their countries through an increasingly uncertain future. Uncertainty looms because of factors such as export and technological dependence (and other reasons we explore in subsequent chapters) and fleeting loyalties of multinational firms.

The nation-state is not about to wither away, but if anything can work to undermine its authority, it would have to be the MNC. Constantly under pressure to lower the costs of operation in order to stay ahead of the competition and faced with continuously improving competitors, MNCs have to find methods and locations that can make them more efficient. If Malaysia is becoming more expensive (perhaps due to its loss of the generalized system of preferences (GSP), a GATT-sanctioned tariff reduction rule), let's move to the Philippines or China or perhaps India. What happens to the capital investment, to expenditures incurred in training labor, to the workers themselves who will lose their jobs and to the government, which perhaps subsidized the facility in the first place? Sources of factor costs can bend over backward in accommodating the peripatetic corporation, but if costs rise (even temporarily), they might as well bid the cost-obsessed MNCs adieu.

The state, though unwilling and perhaps unable to abdicate its preeminent role in politics and economics (both domestic and international), appears to be at the mercy of the global corporation. Unless countries can develop self-sufficiency in providing for their needs and exporting sufficiently to pay for what they need from abroad, companies that can endow nations with the requisite capabilities will hold sway over each nation's direction. Technology and science, the focus of the next chapter, have provided much of the fuel for the rise of Western civilization and—basking in the latter's reflected glory—that of Asia as well. Western technology has been the motive power underlying the "miraculous" economic growth witnessed on the Asian continent. Governments have adopted, invited, induced, borrowed, stolen, imitated, licensed or modified technology by providing fertile ground on which it can be planted. Low-interest or interest-free loans for technology acquisition, assistance in finalizing license agreements, forming consortia to share foreign know-how and the establishment of technology and science parks are strategies that governments have adopted to learn from abroad and build upon that knowledge. The research and development skills needed to conceive of, manufacture and market new products are typically inseparable from the corporations responsible for them. The days when companies would be eager to license technologies to realize immediate gains are long gone. Most companies are seeking either to invest in new plant and equipment or to enter into an alliance with a local partner, the former if they are assured of a market (domestic or export) and if factor conditions are favorable, while joint ventures are most common for gaining market access or if factor conditions are uncertain. Technology is clearly a highly prized possession, and companies are loath to part with it. Governments must, therefore, help develop it indigenously or offer greater inducements to global firms to locate within their borders or to not relocate elsewhere. Against their will and by the nature of the development process itself, some Asian countries' factors are becoming less attractive, while other nations' are gaining ground. Figure 3.1 illustrates a typology arraying factor levels against source of technology with a view to understanding the types of strategies nations might (and do) pursue to stay one step ahead of twinkle-toed multinationals.

The variable "resource levels" encompasses many dimensions; labor and material costs and availabilities, access to capital and to market capacity, tax rates and government incentives and subsidies are the more significant among them. Obviously, some of these dimensions may oppose one another (e.g., labor costs may be low, but there may be a higher degree of unrest, or the local market may be limited in size, and so on). Any conclusions drawn on the basis of this typology have to enunciate specific resources included to carry any face validity. Technology is classified as being either local or foreign, local depending on whether the technology needed is available locally (even if it was originally imported), or whether the specific technology needed has to come from abroad. Clearly, every nation-state would like to be in cell 3, while multinationals are looking for countries in 4. In fact, MNCs would like countries to stay in 4, that is, in a position of technological subservience. Some of modern Asia's success stories have been occupants of cell 4; some still are. China, the Philippines and perhaps Thailand, Indonesia and Malaysia are here, though Malaysia is attempting to move into cell 3 by internalizing the technologies it has experienced over two decades through foreign investments. Malaysia, incidentally, is also drifting upward due to increased wage rates, rising labor expectations and the rather small size of its market. Consequently, it has to adopt the twin

Figure 3.1
Technology Strategies and Resource Levels

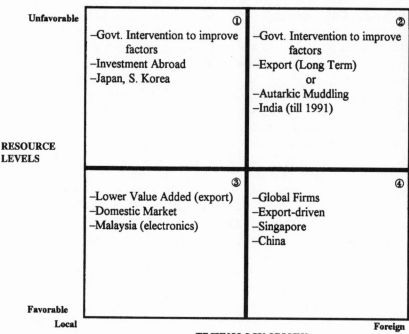

strategies of exports of high value-added products (e.g., audio/video equip-ment) even after the MNCs leave, combined with establishing facilities in countries with more favorable factor conditions. Cell 1 countries, which are faced with less favorable resource levels at home, *must* invest abroad, a strategy that Japanese, Korean, Taiwanese and even some Thai firms are adopting. Nations with large potential markets—China, India and Indo-nesia come to mind—are relatively better placed than smaller nations to weather the problems created by reduced factor attractiveness. Even if costs rise, and economic/political uncertainties intensify, the market's capacity will tend to keep them in the lower half of the cross-classification, allowing them, in a sense, to have their technological cake and eat it, too. They can absorb and adopt foreign technologies to strike out on their own in lower value-added products while continuing as client states for MNCs where they are technologically deficient. Cell 2, becoming rapidly depopulated, requires conscious strategies for resource improvement in order to attract foreign technology and investment, moving toward an export orientation in the longer term. Obdurate governments that wish to remain self-sufficient in technology and not change their policies even slightly will continue to muddle through autarkically, as India did for nearly three decades, while its neighbors addressed their technological inferiority and left India in the dust. Recently, India has moved downward on the diagram, joining the vast majority of its neighbors in migration from cell 2 to cell 4, a journey that will eventually carry them to cell 3 and ultimately to technological mastery—though perhaps only in selected industries—and a higher standard of living.

The state, whether we label it developmental, catalytic, strong or addicted, is still the helmsman behind Asian growth strategies. By entering into alliances such as growth triangles and regional associations, countries attempt to improve their bargaining position vis-à-vis one another, and relative to other nations—especially in the West and Japan—which are becoming increasingly anxious (or is it paranoid?) that their dominant position is being eroded. Multinational corporations, in their worldwide hunt for profits, are constantly jockeying for position with governments, trying to extract all the concessions and market access they possibly can without surrendering their technological advantage. We now turn our attention to that technological advantage, what is being done to narrow it, the modus operandi and the efficacy of technological catch-up in Asia.

NOTES

1. Lester Thurow, *The Future of Capitalism* (New York: Penguin, 1996), pp. 97–98. As Thurow points out, those in the 65-plus age group receive over 40% of their income from the government. Of total tax revenues, the welfare state combined with interest payments consumes 60% and will absorb all tax revenues by the year 2013 if no action is taken.

2. Ibid., p. 104. The fact that government spending on the elderly is nine times the amount spent on children is one indicator that priorities need to be reordered. A balanced budget is no more than a hesitant beginning.

3. Though capitalism has traditionally been myopic, preferring to invest where returns are most likely and immediate, the experience of East Asian countries and the rising income disparity in the United States appear to be pushing the administration in this country toward making massive investments in education.

4. The role of Chinese networks in East and Southeast Asia is presented capably in works such as the East Asia Analytical Unit's *Overseas Chinese Business Networks in Asia* (Commonwealth of Australia, 1995).

5. Francis Fukuyama, *Trust* (London: Penguin, 1995). The linkages between family, society and government are explored at greater length in Chapter 6.

6. Kenichi Ohmae, *The End of the Nation State* (New York: Free Press, 1995), pp. 46–53. Though the Japanese have historically not demurred about subsidizing services provided to remote or revenue-poor areas, this willingness may be coming to an end.

7. Jim Rohwer, *Asia Rising* (New York: Touchstone, 1995), pp. 261–77. The rapid growth of Asian economies could face a formidable roadblock in infrastructural inadequacies, as Rohwer emphasizes.

8. Trevor Matthews and John Ravenhill, "Strategic Trade Policy: The Northeast Asian Experience," in Andrew Macintyre (ed.), *Business and Government in Industrializing Asia* (Ithaca, N.Y.: Cornell University Press, 1994), p. 40.

9. See, for instance, William Greider, *One World, Ready or Not* (New York: Simon and Schuster, 1997), p. 86.

10. Ibid., p. 396.

11. Ibid., pp. 394–96. The phenomenon is not limited to Indonesia, Malaysia or South Korea (where the president's son was indicted in 1997 for corruption). China's communists, too, are intensely nepotistic despite the ideological mumbo-jumbo they mouth in praise of socialism.

12. Nicholas Kristof and Sheryl WuDunn's (*China Wakes* [New York: Random House, 1994], pp. 186–209) characterization of the political system as a "rotting state" carries within it the contradictions inherent to party control in a liberal economic regime whose institutions are created and monitored by the state.

13. The autarkic regimen imposed on the Indian economy from 1947 until 1991 (see Rohwer, *Asia Rising*, as well as *The Economist*'s "Survey of India," February 22, 1997, pp. 24–26) has created an isolationist mind-set masquerading as self-reliance among politicians, bureaucrats, domestic firms and even the populace, each to serve its own interests or allay its biggest concerns (Greider, *One World, Ready or Not*, pp. 394–96).

14. MNCs' ability to shift operations to lower-cost locations leads to a tolerance for primitive working conditions and a harsh repression of labor organizations in many emerging nations. To Greider, factories so organized are reminiscent of Blake's "dark satanic mills" (*One World, Ready or Not*, pp. 333–59).

15. Ibid., p. 137.

16. Ohmae's (*The End of the Nation State*) point is that as portions of emerging countries develop rapidly, they generate stronger ties to the global economy than to the domestic one. Countries are powerless in the face of globalization, Ohmae argues (pp. 72–78).

17. Arrayed against the nation-state are the twin forces of jihad (tendencies to focus on special, narrow interests) and of McWorld, the interests of the global corporation. Benjamin Barber in *Jihad vs. McWorld* (New York: Ballantine, 1996) posits that while the reason for McWorld's tense relationship with the nation-state is obvious, jihad is inimical to nationhood because the former seeks to serve parochial (i.e., narrow) or provincial (i.e., regional) interests. The tendency to use violence in the pursuit of its ends makes dealing with the forces of jihad more risky than it would be to do business with global firms, even ones with interests inimical to those of the state. Controlling parochialism and provincialism is a high priority in China, according to Barber, and has led to strict state control of political and social institutions (pp. 165–70, 184–90).

18. The transnational character of television, music and amusement centers (e.g., theme parks, malls and movie halls) is given extensive treatment by Barber (ibid.), in support of his contention that the pervasive and deep-rooted influence of cultural (particularly of American origin) products counters and yet, in a perverse way, sometimes spawns jihad.

19. The burgeoning influence of the media worldwide combined with the accelerating concentration in the "infotainment" industry makes the standardization of tastes and behaviors among the masses in the developed world, on one hand, and

the elites in the advanced countries, on the other, far easier for MNCs to achieve (ibid., pp. 137–51).

20. Ohmae suggests that managers need to adopt "zebra strategies," identifying similarities in taste, spending power, and so on among parts of a country as well as among parts of different countries, the better to serve regions with divergent needs and purchasing capabilities (Ohmae, *The End of the Nation State*, pp. 22–23, 101–10).

21. World Bank, *The East Asian Miracle* (New York: Oxford University Press, 1993), pp. 29–32.

22. While per capita income ratios between the SEZs and the rest of China have been estimated to be of the order of 5 or 6, Ohmae puts the peak at around 20 (ibid., p. 74). See also Rohwer's estimate of the floating population (*Asia Rising*, p. 154).

23. See Edward Chen and Anna Ho, "Southern China Growth Triangle: An Overview," in Myo Thant, Min Tang, and Hiroshi Kahazin (eds.), *Growth Triangles in Asia* (Hong Kong: Oxford University Press, 1994), pp. 29–72.

24. Singapore's desire to leverage its technological base (obtained by offering inducements to foreign MNCs to locate there) by utilizing the skill and low-cost manpower base as well as export market access, available to Malaysia and Indonesia, is discussed in detail in S. Kumar, "Johor-Singapore-Riau Growth Triangle: A Model of Subregional Cooperation," in Thant et al., *Growth Triangles in Asia*, pp. 175–217.

25. *The Economist*, March 22, 1997.

26. See, for instance, Rohwer, *Asia Rising*, pp. 100–101.

27. APEC's inability to commit itself to meaningful action or deadlines is well known. Rohwer (ibid., p. 101) remarks on member countries' vacillation at their 1994 meeting. The 1996 meeting held in Manila with great fanfare was no different.

28. In spite of the Preferential Treaty Arrangement among SAARC members, the hostility of two of its larger members (India and Pakistan) hinders meaningful action (Subhash Jain and Peruez Ghauri, "Indian Ocean Rim Trade Bloc: Prospects and Problems," *The International Executive* 38, No. 5 [September/October 1996]: 583–97).

29. *The General Agreement on Tariffs and Trade*, Darden School Publication No. UVA-G-0342 (Charlottesville, Va.: Darden, 1988).

30. *The World Trade Organization: Toward Freer Trade or World Bureaucracy*, Publication No. 9-795-149 (Cambridge: Harvard Business School Press, 1995).

4

Technology and Creativity:
The Struggle Ahead

John McPhee, literary geologist extraordinaire, in his aptly titled book, *The Control of Nature*, recounts three fascinating tales of our continuing attempt to subjugate nature.[1] The cameos he presents to the reader in his inimitable style are

- the Corps of Engineers' ongoing struggle to prevent the Atchafalaya—a tributary of the Mississippi—from capturing its senior partner, stranding New Orleans and Baton Rouge and leaving the industrial belt known as the "American Ruhr" high and dry. When stated in economic terms—the price of not stemming the outflow from the Mississippi was reckoned to be nothing less than the loss of the United States' preeminence in world trade and competitiveness—the conclusion was, and is, inescapable. Nature, as McPhee puts it, "had become an enemy of the state" (p. 7) and must be engaged in uneasy combat.

- the fight against volcanic eruptions on the island of Vestmannaeyjar in Iceland. Rather than abandon the island, salvaging as much as possible in retreat, the residents, led by an iconoclastic physicist, aimed water hoses at the lava flow. As the volume of water pumped increased, the rock that formed at the leading edge of the lava helped first slow it and then redirect it away from residential buildings and the harbor. Against one of the lava flows around 30 million gallons of seawater were pumped, solidifying a volume of basalt "about the size of Yankee Stadium" (p. 140). Using high-capacity pumps and endless resolve and ignoring the snickering that accompanied their initial efforts, the lava warriors forced nature down—at least for a while.

- the unremitting struggle being waged in and around Los Angeles to deal with the numerous, often catastrophic *debris flows* that occur in the San Gabriel Mountains. Debris flows contain material of varying sizes, some as large as cars. Some, indeed, *are* cars. Frequently, owners of houses built in the mountains overlooking

Los Angeles find streams and their massive contents all over their living rooms or find their living rooms in the valley below. Fire and rain are the twin original causes of debris flows. Fires cause the powdery soil to tumble into streambeds and coalesce into bigger and bigger chunks of rock that impede the flow of water. When enough head is built up, the blocked steam bursts out with explosive force. The containment of debris flows is therefore an unceasing fight—the formation of highly flammable chaparral combined with torrential rain occurs periodically, though, thankfully, not frequently—and the effects, rather than the causes, are all that can be countered. In the confrontation with nature, underground conduits and open channels are the foot soldiers. They help carry the water that would have otherwise been transported by rivers and streams. The heavy firepower is, however, provided by *debris basins*, which are huge pits, hemispherical in shape and sometimes as large as a stadium, scooped out of the mountains. The debris flow enters these basins, hopefully never to emerge.

Technology, in a manner of speaking, uses nature's ideas and processes to develop devices to help us rise above nature itself. One of the greatest achievements of science has been the demystification of our lives and of nature itself. Instead of a blind belief that all phenomena and occurrences are the result of direct divine intervention, we tend to look for explanations rooted in our experience or in principles we have enunciated. Volcanoes, earthquakes, comets, fossil records, diseases and illnesses are attributed to factors whose impact is measured with as much precision as possible.

Ever since the Industrial Revolution gathered steam in England, exploded across Europe and later took the New World by storm, the notion that our inventions, the creatures of our mind, can help us overcome limitations placed on us by nature has held us in its tight embrace. Need shelter against the elements? Better housing designs, improved materials or superior techniques of construction are the answer. How about curing large numbers of people of potentially fatal diseases? Medical technology has some of the solutions. If you want to travel more comfortably and faster, you can take your pick of a variety of luxury cars, or, if oceans must be bridged, you have your choice of airlines. Few will dispute that one of the West's enduring contributions to the record of human achievement and even survival lies in technology and its products. (There is, of course, the downside that we can, without much ado, destroy ourselves, too, but as with all technological articulations, the choice is ours.) Our ability to deal with, and control, nature is intimately linked to how well we understand it. The pragmatic discoveries of technology are interwoven with the spirit of inquiry of science. Obviously, people have been using tools and technical means to better their lot since time immemorial. The plow, the wheel, the ax and the boat were all familiar to, and employed by, most of the ancient civilizations known to us. Inventions such as these predated the advent of scientific inquiry and methodology. It was, however, only when a collective desire and ability to understand nature more fully took hold in Europe in the sixteenth and seventeenth centuries that the interplay between know-how and know-why became overt and productive.[2] When the acceleration of a falling object, the composition of the atmosphere, the properties of gasses, the behavior of light and sound and a host of other phenomena were becoming better and more widely comprehended, the rate of invention and innovation picked up considerably. Better yet, since they were now based on a rational foundation, not on intuition or trial and error, the devices could be more readily improved and be made more reliable. Science elevated technology to levels it had not reached before, and technology, in its turn, helped science through the development of better machines (pumps to create a vacuum, clocks to measure time accurately, glass to withstand high pressure etc.).

Almost in lockstep with technology, yet fulfilling a different set of functions, are the activities collectively labeled management. Management encompasses decisions and actions as diverse as Cyrus McCormick's innovative installment payment plan for the mechanical reaper developed at International Harvester, Toyota's implementation of just-in-time manufacturing, largely utilizing existing manufacturing hardware, and Kodak's decision to export its technology and thus take the fight to its rivals (primarily Fuji). Management introduces technology and, hence science to the everyday world. The relative isolation and highly specialized pursuits of the scientist stand in clear contrast to the evaluation of relevance and of potential demand and the configuring of human, material and information resources that informs managerial actions. Financing has to be arranged (internally or by selling stock/incurring debt), raw materials have to be located and ordered and the product has to be designed, engineered, manufactured and transported. Above all, customers must be satisfied and satisfied continuously. The organization of these varied resources on an ongoing basis is the magic of management, the culmination of the process of science and technology,[3] for, without applications on a large scale and in a way that touches the lives of the bulk of the population, science itself would wither on the vine. The scientific revolution, it is true, occurred without any guarantee of its discoveries being useful or even relevant. After all, Copernicus did not speculate and theorize about the center of the known universe with any known commercial intent. Neither did Galileo, Newton, Maxwell or Lavoisier visualize the impact his work would have, individually and collectively, on life on the planet.[4] Nevertheless, without the Industrial Revolution, the scientific revolution may well have sputtered to a halt. Science that is known to the few and accessible to even fewer remains an esoteric occupation, clearly separated from the lives of common people and therefore denied the vitalizing force of public opinion—the examples of ancient Greece, China, India and similar old civilizations that often reached scientific dead ends buttress this point.[5] The pre-1991 Soviet Union might seem to offer a counterexample—that is, of a totalitarian

Figure 4.1
The STM Symbiosis

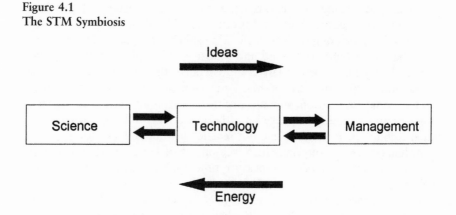

society that undoubtedly made noteworthy progress in the sciences. However, Soviet science, lacking the (eventual) demand pull of a market economy, resulted in technologies that often tended to be less than sophisticated. This strongly suggests that where the energy—economic, political and moral—of society is denied to science in the long term, particularly in the form of consumer demand and competitive forces, both science and technology are likely to develop only in areas where an external challenge can be created, for example, the threat of attack or of humiliation (similar to the effect the launching of the sputnik had on the United States) by a rival nation.

Therefore, while individual scientists and inventors hone their theories, ideas, products and techniques, managers are responsible for pulling the various pieces together to form a viable and beneficial whole. Today, as has been true particularly through the past two centuries, the ability of management to secure public approbation, in the form of demand for products/services, is essential to the symbiotic relationship between science, technology and management (STM) depicted in Figure 4.1. The forward linkage among the three, through the medium of ideas—products, processes, attitudes and methodology—is the one more commonly cited and lauded. However, the reverse linkage is equally important if the development of new technologies is to be economically viable. Scientific research, moreover, not only needs to be funded but, equally important (and this is particularly true in the case of experimental science), requires highly specialized equipment such as linear accelerators, metals of extreme purity, high-resolution radio telescopes and so on. The energy generated by market demand and public esteem sustains technologies and the science they are based on as much as the ideas of the latter result in stimulating technological and economic activity in the first place.

The marriage of science, technology and management in Europe and

America was founded on *democratic principles* and the emergence of the *free enterprise* system. Without the acceptance of egalitarian ideas, the notion that *everyone* deserves to participate in the sharing of wealth would have been stillborn, if it had ever been conceived. The possibility of wealth dispersion naturally best came to fruition when the creators of wealth participated in its distribution—through the mechanism of the free market.[6] A third factor was essential to supplement political freedom and economic competition. Organizations were crucial to achieve resource consolidation and to best serve the market's needs. Individual scientists and inventors, therefore, honed their theories, ideas, products and techniques. However, consolidating and uniting the various pieces into a viable and beneficial whole were, and are, the charge placed upon managers everywhere. While the nature and future of the role played by science and technology in Asia are our focus in this chapter, Asian management is the subject of the next.

The inability of civilizations like those of China and India to rise beyond the level of affluence they had achieved while Europe was still embroiled in the long era of stagnation known as the Dark Ages has long puzzled scholars. One of the explanations offered for the phenomenon is that Europe emerged from its extended seclusion with a sharpened sense of curiosity.[7] Tales of strange and mystical lands brought back by returning crusaders, for instance, whetted the desire of the common people and of would-be explorers to find out more about the world beyond their familiar shores. Technological improvements like changes in ship design and the availability of better compasses helped sailors go farther than they would have dared to earlier, while the enterprise and encouragement of rulers like Prince Henry the Navigator provided the financial backing that venturesome travelers—who did not know exactly where they were going or what they were likely to find—so sorely needed.[8] When one considers the extent of ignorance that persisted well into the sixteenth century of what lay beyond the known parts of Europe and of the types of human and other living beings one might encounter if and when one made land and the low likelihood of surviving long sea voyages, it is a wonder that anyone ever embarked on these long expeditions. Undoubtedly, the desire to chart the uncharted, to discover the unknown and mysterious was not the sole motivation of the intrepid initiators, organizers and leaders of these trips to distant lands. The urge to proselytize and to convert the "heathen" to Christianity was surely a potent driving force, as was the search for ancient, possibly vast treasures to be won by those courageous enough to blaze a pioneering trail.[9] The questing spirit, the search for lands of mystery, was, no doubt, at least in part, spurred by narrow considerations of making new converts and more money, both of which purposes clearly reached a pinnacle with the Spanish conquests in Central and South America. However, to claim that spiritual and monetary incentives were what ignited the age of discovery would be to ignore the sense of an unshackling of minds and bodies that pervaded much of Europe when its period of seclusion ended. After the land route to Asia had been closed in the thirteenth century, the desire was strong, three centuries later, to reestablish links with the fabled lands travelers like Marco Polo had written about. The mental expansion that Europe was experiencing in a geographical sense was paralleled by a conceptual expansion. Scientific pursuits were beginning to engage inquiring minds all over Europe. Supernatural explanations no longer held sway as the methodological rigor of the observation-hypothesis-testing cycle took hold. Copernicus turned Ptolemaic astronomy on its head, just as, almost simultaneously, explorers on terra firma dramatically altered Ptolemy's map of the world. The possibility of a sea route to the East around the African continent—which refuted Ptolemy's view that impenetrable land barriers lay where we now know the Indian Ocean to be—fired the imagination of royalty and peasant alike.

The Chinese and the Indians were by no means timid landlubbers themselves.[10] Chinese vessels had sailed without much ado in the South China Sea and ranged as far afield, till the fifteenth century, as the Straits of Malacca. When the eunuch admiral Cheng Ho undertook his first expedition to India and beyond in the fifteenth century, he was merely upholding an established seafaring tradition in his country. What he did when he got to far-off lands and how his voyages were viewed back at home were clear indicators of the attitude to discovery common to China at that time. The admiral, who was at the head of a large, intimidating fleet, impressed the natives of the places he visited (e.g., the eastern coast of Africa, parts of northeastern India and what is now Sri Lanka) with the immense force he commanded. However, rather than demand tribute from them or seek to alter their belief system, the Chinese merely left behind gifts and treasures as (expensive) calling cards and remembrances. No doubt, one can contend that this action reflects a nobility never displayed by the Europeans. On the other hand, this generosity may be interpreted as an act of patronizing superiority. The Chinese felt they were so superior to the peoples they encountered that they gave mementos and treasures away to emphasize their civilization's stature. The Middle Kingdom (which meant that it was closer to paradise than all others on earth) considered itself to be a nation apart, a nation that had nothing to learn from any other. The lack of a desire to interact also reflected an unwillingness to learn, a conviction that all that one needed to know was to be found within the nation's borders. Visitors and court residents from Europe only added to this complacency. The Jesuits, whose learning impressed the emperor and his nobles, were particularly grievous offenders in this regard.[11] Matteo Ricci, for instance, waxed eloquent about the numerous technological attainments of the Chinese, creating the impression that he was living in the midst of a vibrant, growing civilization. While the wisdom and the administrative attainments of the Confucian system were never in doubt, the fact that the practical achievements, the ability to transform invention into useful artifact, had atrophied was generally ignored. Of course, the Jesuits were beholden to their hosts for their safety and comfort and were engaged in a "civilizing mission." That is, like most Western visitors to exotic lands in the Middle Ages, the Jesuits wished to convert the Chinese nobility to Christianity, which would, in their view, improve their lot in this life as well. As more visitors began to make their way to the Middle Kingdom, however, the accounts they returned with of the state of affairs were not entirely complimentary.[12] Many spoke of China as a nation in decline or, at best, one with a brilliant past and a stagnant present. Some observers pointed to the Confucian respect for ancestors and tradition as the major impediment standing in China's path to achieve parity with the West. It was also believed by some that Christianity had been the differentiating factor between Western dynamism and Chinese stupor. Where India was concerned, Western praise was nowhere near as copious and unstinting.[13] Most visitors and scholars, while conceding that Indian philosophy had, indeed, been wide-ranging and percipient, excoriated the elite and a society that had rested on its laurels for centuries. In any event, Indian achievements in technology, unlike the Chinese, had been sparse, being rooted more in myth than in reality. Beyond speculating that, based on descriptions provided in epics such as the *Mahabharata* and *Ramayana,* ancient India had developed weapons based on advanced technology—a claim that is echoed to this very day by die-hard fundamentalists and obscurantists—India could offer little evidence of technological prowess to the searching gaze Europeans directed at it. As in the case of China, an explanation offered for the apparent decay of Indian civilization was a societal one—that Brahmins, the upper caste in the straitjacket of stratification, had jealously guarded the store of knowledge they had accumulated through the years. They had neither helped disseminate ideas, thus increasing the likelihood of improvements, nor encouraged creativity among themselves. India and China had become smug, inward-looking and unwilling (or unable) to admit that they could learn from the rest of the world.[14] The authoritarian, elitist nature of the regimes ruling both countries was also viewed as a stumbling block to either nation's ever becoming a force that Europeans would have to take seriously. Clocks, for instance, had been developed in China at about almost the same time they had started finding favor in Europe's monasteries to time matins, vespers and other daily prayers more precisely. In China, however, clocks remained little more than curiosities at the court, fascinating baubles with no practical purpose.[15] In Europe, on the other hand, the use of clocks spread to civilian life initially when clock towers were installed in public squares and, subsequently, when ordinary citizens wished to order their days in a more disciplined and predictable manner. The sense of time and punctuality and the ability to plan and even control one's daily life better that resulted from the popular use of clocks and timepieces cannot be exaggerated. Regularity of work schedules raised productivity and created a mind-set that set the lifestyles of industrial organization apart from farming communities. No such distinction emerged in Asia until the late nineteenth century in Japan, and even that was borrowed from the West. The fact that inventions like the compass, gunpowder and paper did not lead to further developments, by-products, a thriving spirit of creativity and widespread application only meant that each invention was a blind alley. The interconnectedness that was to be a feature of technological change in Europe in the seventeenth century and thereafter was nowhere in evidence. Indifference to the common good was surely one of the main contributory factors. The absence of the scientific method was undoubtedly as significant.[16] The tradition-shattering ideas of Copernicus, Newton and Kepler were no accident—they were the result of looking at the world in a completely different way. Theories that did not hold water were abandoned, and new ones that did fit, however outrageous and incredible, were adopted. As the willingness to jettison old ideas grew, a constant desire to debunk the accepted wisdom became a part of scientific methodology. "Falsification," as Popper termed it, almost became an end in itself.[17] A theory had to be stated in testable, that is, falsifiable terms, which served as a powerful inducement to scientists to improve upon the explanatory power of existing theories. "Normal science," in the vocabulary of Kuhn, was no more than a paradigm awaiting to be overthrown.[18] The "creative destruction" of the technology innovation process that Schumpter wrote about is no less a feature of the scientific process as well. It was not a trait that Asian civilizations displayed in the past. They do not appear to have acquired or cultivated this vital ability even in the waning years of the twentieth century.

The Japanese were clearly the earliest among Asian nations to realize that the growing industrial muscle of Europe was vesting it with a military, economic and political edge that, if ignored, would get only progressively larger and more difficult to overcome. Japan decided, almost a full century before any other country on the Asian continent, that it would learn all it could about science and technology from the source itself. The best and brightest were dispatched to various European universities to imbibe, and return with, the new knowledge. Some of the returnees went to the extent of sporting European attire—dressing in top hat and tailcoat for formal occasions—while others became aficionados of Western classical music and the opera. Pragmatism, a trait of the nation to this day, made initiation of successful foreigners a virtue, helping suppress any qualms over the admission of inadequacy. In that sense, too, Japan has served as a role model for the rest of Asia, which has realized that if overcoming a deficiency requires emulation of, and learning from, successful nations, thereby affirming one's backward status, so be it.

Japan learned only too well how effectively technology can be adopted to suit belligerent political ends.[19] Its expansionist ventures in Russia and China in the early twentieth century and the aggressiveness of its actions during the Second World War are evidence of that. As a result, however, not only was much of Japan laid to waste by aerial bombardment and by the twin nuclear explosions, but Japan's image in much of Asia lay in tatters. Having tried by force to create a "Great East Asia Co-Prosperity Sphere" (a fond dream of Japanese politicians before the war), the Japanese had no economy and no allies in 1945. The country's postwar recovery and the government's critical role in it are too well known to bear retelling.

MITI, the acknowledged guardian of the interests of business in Japan, played a prominent role in advancing technology within corporations and creating technological capability in the country itself. MITI accomplished this in several ways. Initially, recognizing that Japan had much ground to cover to be even mentioned in the same breath, technologically speaking as its Western allies, MITI allowed the importation of technologies it considered critical to likely future "winner" industries.[20] Licensing was the most common route followed, with MITI taking the lead in negotiating the terms of the purchase. Whether the transaction was concluded with Texas Instruments or Dupont, MITI bargained on price and on the terms of transfer. The ministry was also very active in ensuring that the licensed technology went a long way. Rather than allow competing firms to bid the price up with foreign sellers or allow each firm independently to acquire similar technologies, MITI acted as the architect and crafter of Japan's technology strategy. True, the Japanese excelled in adopting and implementing innovations from abroad. Textiles, shipbuilding, motorcycles, steel, automobiles, consumer electronics—the list of industries targeted, entered and conquered by the Japanese through imitation is long and well known to anyone familiar with world business. But, to give credit where credit is due, Japanese firms were not, and are not, mere purloiners of ideas. They did not—indeed, they could not—hope to absorb techniques and know-how by applying them unchanged to get the better of their erstwhile mentors. In addition to deploying strategic trade theory and strategic technology, the Japanese actively pursued the achievement of comparative advantage. They found it in the gradual, cumulative process technology improvements they instituted in numerous manufacturing facilities across a range of industries. Admittedly, low labor cost proved to be a boon early on, which, coupled with an undervalued yen, gave them a leg up on manufacturers from advanced countries. But as the yen rose in value, along with wage rates, the Japanese did not surrender their comparative advantage in the process of manufacturing. Indeed, over the past two decades that, if anything, has served as the flagship for Japanese firms' apparent invincibility abroad (buttressed, of course, by the efforts of a partisan government). Centralized and mammoth plants established by Nippon Steel and Fuji Film generated tremendous economies of scale and initiated price competition in their respective industries, a strategy their rivals were un-prepared, unable and reluctant to emulate. Canon and Sharp reverse-engineered Xerox's copiers to see exactly what made them tick, after which they redesigned them to make them more compact and user-friendly.[21] They also used the concept of design for manufacturability (DFM), ena-bling the product to be assembled more easily while reducing its cycle time. Toyota, on the other hand, questioned the very basis on which success in automobile mass production had been founded. Realizing that large batch production stood in the way of providing product variety, Toyota's engi-neers set about dethroning this deity from its pedestal.[22] They wanted a process that was both flexible and efficient. They found it in the concept known as just-in-time (JIT) manufacturing, utilizing the technique termed *kanban* (card). The latter dictates that material be produced only when needed by the next operation, which minimized inventory and slack or extra time, as well as cycle times. Since changeovers must be done more quickly, more customization is possible, making the manufacturing process more responsive to users' needs. Most manufacturing innovations adopted by the Japanese featured a high degree of employee involvement in the technology change process. Consultation with the workforce, at least in regard to modes of implementation, and the use of teams cutting across formal organizational lines made technology everyone's business, not just the concern of engineers in comfortable offices far removed from the grime and the sweat of the shop floor. Total quality management (TQM), based on the principle of minimizing variation but brought to fruition through the participation of all employees, further exemplifies the notion of tech-nology as a grassroots activity.[23] While Chapter 6 takes a closer look at Japanese management practices, it is worth stating here that the transfer of technological hardware is but a part, perhaps a minor part, of the road to technology catch-up. Devising ways in which the technology can be appro-priately adapted before being adopted is critical to success in the transfer process, and the Japanese have shown an unparalleled ability to stretch techniques, tools and methods beyond the purposes originally envisioned for them.

Process improvements, though they account for much of the initial suc-cess corporations like Toyota, Matsushita and Toshiba achieved, do not tell the entire technology story of Japan's rebirth. Far from it. As they speeded along the process technology fast lane, whizzing by their erstwhile mentors, Japan's leading corporations were reminded by MITI that the national strategy had to be modified from catch-up to leap-ahead. Firms in Japan have responded by escalating their research and development expen-ditures to levels almost matching those obtained in other advanced nations. R&D spending hovers around 2.5% of GDP in Japan, the United States and Germany and at slightly lower levels in the U.K., France and Italy.[24] Although the American R&D effort matches that of the Japanese in relative terms, being almost double in absolute dollar amounts, a significant portion of the R&D dollar in the United States is allocated to defense needs.[25] At the peak of the cold war, around two-thirds of what the government spent on R&D was directed to military purposes. The proportion is now around 50%, still a considerable sum. The nondefense R&D to GDP ratio in Japan is nearly 40% higher than that in the United States, indicating that the latter still spends heavily on military-oriented R&D. While civilian spin-offs from such R&D are certainly possible, the difference in these ratios tells us that the United States at 2% is clearly behind its major international rivals, Japan (2.7%) and Germany (2.4%), in the level of nondefense R&D proportionate to the country's GDP. The U.S. government provides around $60 billion in R&D funding, of which over $30 billion is devoted to defense purposes. The Japanese government provides only 20% of the funds needed for R&D, with industry in Japan contributing over 75% of the financing.[26] The comparable contribution by corporations in the United States is a little over 50%. The difference in defense-related R&D in the two nations needs little elaboration or explanation. The United States, bearing the brunt of the struggle against Russian and Chinese communism, built up a vast corporate-government alliance, the defense contractors often "capturing" their customers based on capabilities in R&D, manufacturing and contractual relationships cemented over the years. While the monopsonistic situation should have resulted in the government's calling the shots, the fact was, and is, that companies such as McDonnell Douglas, Lockheed, Martin Marietta and Grumman built unassailable competitive advantages in specific weapons and equipment systems, making it almost impossible to dislodge them. Of course, the Department of Defense (DOD) does try to cultivate alternative suppliers, but, given the high R&D expenditures involved, the absence of a mass market and exclusion of foreign firms from bidding due to security concerns, there is typically little competition in this single-customer market. Inefficiencies are bound to become a feature of corporate functioning, particularly where cost plus contracts are the norm. Its responsibilities as leader of the noncommunist world, therefore, committed the United States to spending heavily on defense, an expenditure that could not be controlled through the use of market forces or by a rigorous insistence on efficiency in operations. Defense spending, however, is only half of the government R&D picture. The other dimension to public funds used for R&D arises from the reluctance of corporations, whose gaze is firmly fixed on product, service or process, to spend time or money on basic research. Advancing the frontiers of knowledge is all very well, but if the goal is undefined, and the means unclear, companies with impatient shareholders are not going to be overly eager to undertake this sort of exploratory activity. The government has to take the lead here, and the fact that the Japanese government spends far less than its American counterpart is an indicator of both frugality and myopia.[27] The frugality is made much of by authors who trumpet the fact that the Japanese government is the source of less than 1% of industrial R&D spending there, whereas the U.S. government provides nearly 20% of the R&D funds for industry in this country. Half of the latter is for defense, as noted earlier, the remainder being mainly for basic research. Japanese efforts in basic research have therefore been negligible since corporations are loath to spend on a form of R&D that has no obvious application. Over three-quarters of Japanese R&D is for development—product improvements, researching of better materials, process refinements and so on. All of this goes to support the incremental, continuous improvement methodologies so highly valued by the Japanese. (The corresponding figure for development in the United States is 60%.)[28]

The greater emphasis accorded to basic research or research that is more contiguous to science than to the marketplace in the United States relative to Japan emerges from a look at the science linkage or the average number of references to scientific literature in patent applications. The U.S. rate is double the linkage of the Asian region (dominated by Japan) and the European community. However, in two other technology performance indicators, the United States lags behind Japan. The current impact index (CII) measures the frequency with which a country's recent patents are cited by all the year's patents, while the technology cycle time (TCT) measures the median age in years of references cited in the patent applications. The Japanese edge in both the CII and TCT reinforces their penchant for advancing inch by inch through numerous marginal adjustments. Obviously, this results in the well-known phenomenon of American firms' doing the conceptual and applied research that the Japanese profitably develop into a successful product.[29] However, in the 1990s, corporate spending on development has increased at about 1% per year, reaching a total of $71 billion in 1995. With the curtailing of government support for development (the bulk of which went for defense needs anyway), firms are picking up the slack and directing their attention to commercial ends. This could mean that it could get progressively more difficult for Japanese firms to be first to the marketplace with products originally conceived and designed elsewhere. The "cuckoo syndrome" (the cuckoo makes another bird's nest its own), which allowed the Japanese to successfully manufacture and market hand-held calculators, VCRs, color televisions and numerous other such products, may be running its course. Certainly, the Japanese are quick to spot ideas that will fly and have been willing to risk their money on concepts as yet unproven. But the increased importance being attached to development in the United States and the slowdown in the Japanese economy are likely to come together, constraining the traditional forte of the Japanese.

As Reischauer, the former American ambassador to Japan and a longtime admirer of the country and its people, observed, the Japanese are not given to lofty concepts and abstract ideas as are, say, the West and India.[30] Rather, they are down-to-earth, seek tangible applications of ideas and appear less competent than the West at cutting-edge research. Having spent over three decades catching up with America and Europe in technology, the Japanese are discovering they are better suited to gaining on their rivals than pulling ahead and staying ahead—which requires, as we have seen, the willingness and the ability to undertake basic research. The collaborative efforts fostered by MITI worked well during a period when the goals of research in various industries were reasonably clear, and the market leaders—Xerox, Kodak, Phillips, General Electric—were to be emulated and bettered, their products reengineered and improved. But when the task consists of visualizing and *creating* products for which the past is not a reliable guide, success seems to be relatively elusive. Scott Callon offers some fascinating vignettes of attempts at collaboration misfiring badly among elite Japanese firms, particularly in computer-related industries.[31] Getting wind of an IBM plan for very large-scale integration (VLSI), MITI proposed a consortium consisting of NEC, Toshiba, Fujitsu, Hitachi and Mitsubishi to radically upgrade existing Dynamic Random Access Memory (DRAM) capabilities. NTT wanted control of the consortium, but since MITI was charged with overseeing the computer industry, NTT was not given the leadership role. As the MITI effort got under way, however, NTT tried launching its own venture by including some of the same firms already in MITI's consortium. NTT's concern ostensibly was that AT&T had pulled far ahead of Japan, but a nagging desire not to let MITI get too much credit for VLSI may have had something to do with it. MITI, however, managed to sabotage NTT's venture. The two agencies later seemed to bury the hatchet, but it was all *tatemae*, as the Japanese put it, for appearance's sake. MITI was soon to find that there were stormier seas ahead. The consortium members were initially horrified to learn that they would work in joint laboratories and agreed to shared facilities only after being assured that the work done in the labs would be basic research that was too risky and expensive to undertake alone. At any event, only 15% of the work was performed jointly, most labs were dominated by particular firms and the best researchers were rarely nominated to work in partnership with other firms. Though the bulk of the research (85%) was carried out by firms working separately, meaning that 85% of the patents bore only one firm's name, even the little cooperation needed in the common facilities was *tatemae*. Paranoia ran so deep that scientists and engineers often wrote down what they knew at the start of the project to ensure it did not form part of a joint patent or another firm's patent. The precise division of labor among firms also meant, paradoxically enough, that work was often duplicated: members did not want others to steal a march over them by being sole custodians of valuable knowledge. In spite of the high level of distrust that prevailed within the consortium, the VLSI was successful compared to the performance of the other consortia that MITI cobbled together. Seventy percent of the R&D on semiconductors was funded by the consortium, with MITI providing 40% of it. At a time when liberalization was taking place in the semiconductor industry—after insistent U.S. pressure—VLSI reduced dependence on imported equipment even with the elimination of import controls. It also gained the Japanese some breathing room in the face of the perceived threat posed by IBM's planned DRAM enhancements.

The projects conceived by MITI for racing ahead in supercomputers and taking the world by storm with its fifth-generation machines faced more numerous and less superable hurdles.[32] Their outcomes were decidedly discomfiting, if not calamitous, for the firms concerned, even more so for their orchestrator, MITI. Again, one of the driving forces was the fear that IBM was close to developing so-called Josephson junctions, which provided for superior switching times and memories. MITI decided that Japan had to catch up with and overtake Cray, but NEC, Fujitsu and Hitachi were, in a sense, "enemies in the same boat." Fujitsu, which had had some experience with vector superconductors, refused to share any information with the partner-rivals. The latter, therefore, built simulators for compiling. They refused to share their finding with Fujitsu, however, since that would give Fujitsu the complete picture, enabling it to go it alone. Paranoia and distrust reached such peak levels that Hitachi and NEC engineers visiting Fujitsu's plant were not allowed to ride in the same bus as the host's engineers! The goals set for the project at its inception were framed in terms of computing speed, access memory and the incorporation of Josephson junctions and gallium arsenide technology, achieving world leadership status in all three. MITI claimed and proclaimed the supercomputer a success, even though the machine used only 4, rather than the 16, Central Processing Units (CPUs) originally envisaged. The speed test was rigged to achieve the target, using trivial software. The graphics and data flow attainments were run-of-the-mill and brought the consortium up to U.S. standards. The project collapsed, partly because IBM developed junctions that worked at higher temperatures than the Josephson junctions, gallium arsenide did not prove as viable as the improvements achieved in silicon and MITI ran out of money. The fifth-generation venture failed as miserably as the superconductor did, although there was more basic research involved. One faction in MITI wanted the fifth-generation machine to be based on existing systems and principles, while another group desired a radical shift in design. The Ministry of Education (MoE), which bore the responsibility for scientific (basic) research, did not assign any of its people to the project. The focus of the project was on hardware despite the known Japanese deficiencies in software. Again, MITI declared victory, this time by revising the goals after the project had ended in dismal failure. Interagency conflicts were, and continue to be, the bane of collaborative research guided by the government. The Ministry of Education coordinates all scientific endeavors and typically guards its bailiwick jealously. Attempts by MITI or any other arm of the government to "intrude" into its territory is resisted, usurped or torpedoed. Since the MoE is "responsible" for research conducted in academic institutions, and MITI for that pursued by corporations, the twain do not frequently meet. That is, the transfer of basic research to corporations and the communication of corporate needs to scientists are relatively rare, hence, the poor science linkage mentioned earlier. The MoE has, in the 1990s, become slightly less inflexible, allowing researchers from firms to pursue their investigations in universities and offering financial support to promising projects. But the turf battle with MITI is a structural problem that will not disappear unless mechanisms and/or incentives for cooperation between academe and corporate Japan are put in place. Rather than wait for government-initiated moves to stimulate basic research to bear fruit, firms like Hitachi, NGK Insulators, Asaki Chemicals and IBM Japan have set up their own affiliates to pursue research near the interface between science and technology.

Further evidence of the realization among Japanese firms that, in spite of their heroic technological efforts, they have far to go in basic research is provided by their willingness to enter into international strategic technology alliances (ISTA).[33] Though the most numerous ISTAs are between European and American firms—which could retard Japanese efforts at drawing level even more—the number (approximately 170 in 1994) is impressive. The most popular form of ISTA used to be the joint venture with equity participation by the partners but has gradually shifted to nonequity partnerships, sharing risks and technologies but not ownership. The very rationale for the formation of strategic alliances, however, breeds distrust of partners who could become rivals. Boeing, for instance, has increasingly involved Mitsubishi in the design and manufacture of the fuselage for its planes. It is obvious that Mitsubishi has plans to enter the world aircraft industry in the first decade of the next century, but Boeing needs Mitsubishi (both for its know-how and management competencies and because Japanese airlines are valuable customers) almost as much as Mitsubishi needs Boeing. That does not, nevertheless, mean that absolute trust characterizes their relationship.[34] The pathologies that marked the functioning of the VLSI superconductor and fifth-generation consortia are instructive reminders of how far even potential competitors will go (or not go) in cooperating with one another.

Another avenue that can yield rich rewards in staying at the cutting edge of technology is through setting up R&D organizations in the lead nations themselves. The Japanese, for instance, in 1994 owned 219 such facilities in the United States, the bulk of them being in the automobile, computer, software and electronics industries.[35] Biotechnology, chemicals and semiconductors were also targets for Japanese investment. About 10% of R&D funds expended in the United States came from affiliates of foreign companies. The corresponding figure for Japan is 0.1%. The total R&D expenditure in Japan has obviously far outstripped the growth in R&D funds from foreign firms. The need to learn from abroad is still not overpowering or even strong in a society so homogeneous that one might expect the import of ideas would be a high priority.

Technology product exports and imports facilitate the transfer of ideas and techniques as well. The United States is the world's largest exporter of technology. Fully 25% of its exports are of technology products, while only 19% of its imports are for such products, meaning a positive balance of trade in the sector. Information, aerospace and electronics constitute the bulk of the exports from this country, with Japan and Canada each importing about 12% of American technology exports. The "Asian tigers" (Hong Kong, Singapore, Taiwan and South Korea) were, for their size, relatively large importers (17% combined) as well. The bulk of the exports were to Singapore, whose strategy is to develop a comparative advantage in technology as its labor costs rise. (Singapore Airlines' large purchases of Boeing also contributed significantly to the import bill—an outlay that has generated huge revenues for the country.) Singapore, in its turn, also accounted for 11% of U.S. technology imports, with Japan being, by far, the leader with 29%. In fact, Asian countries supplied 65% of the U.S. technology purchases from abroad.[36] The bulk of Japan's exports are in optoelectronics, computers, electronics, computer-integrated manufacturing (CIM) and new materials. The Japanese emphasis on R&D in manufacturing industries accounts for much of their export success. Having farmed out production to facilities in Malaysia, Thailand, China and Indonesia, the Japanese continue with R&D at home. Typically, the Japanese do not part with know-how easily, keeping the high-tech information/telecom technology know-how of products made elsewhere to themselves.[37] The fact that local firms produce most of the components needed for audio systems and cordless phones does not mean that they are equipped to compete with their erstwhile customers. Lacking many stages (manufacturing equipment development, new product development, design principles, modeling and tool design etc.) of the entire value chain needed to create the product, local vendors are hard-pressed to do much on their own. Malaysia's high level of technology exports (around $5 billion) is not, therefore, indicative of its position as technologically powerful but rather of the fact that it is building products incorporating high-technology black boxes (since it does not know much about the most critical component of the final product).[38] Even the Japanese success in exporting high technology to the United States must be placed in proper perspective. The areas most focused upon are, with few exceptions, traditional strengths upon which they are making incremental improvements. For instance, optoelectronics and CIM are nowhere near the basic research frontier, and the work in computers/telecom is typically the result of technology gleaned from world leaders or derived from following in their footsteps.[39] Even Japan—the undisputed technological giant in Asia—is, therefore, hard-pressed to be a pioneer in, and dominate, any industry, nor has it demonstrated the ability to pioneer or even to dominate a family of industries. Japan's problems where science and technology are concerned are magnified greatly for the other relatively advanced countries in Asia—Korea and Taiwan, in particular. That is, their industrial focus is narrow (e.g., semiconductors in Korea, computers in Taiwan), much of their technological prowess is borrowed or the result of incremental improvement, little cutting-edge research is conducted and the importation of technology is not encouraged.[40]

The Korea Institute of Science and Technology, established in 1966, was a recognition by the Korean government earlier in the country's growth cycle that labor-intensive industries would not provide a haven of comparative advantage too long, regardless of how effectively strategic trade or technology was applied. Events proved the government right. As the Japanese started establishing manufacturing footholds in East and Southeast Asia—being welcomed at this time, in marked contrast to their reception in the same countries during the Second World War—Korea's wage advantage slipped dramatically. The government has attempted to address this challenge by establishing research institutes, many clustered together in the Daeduk Science Town, modeled after Tsukaba Science City in Japan. Incentives have been provided for private firms to pursue R&D, too. However, Korea's R&D expenditure is about equivalent to that of one of the largest American firms, and it is highly dependent on Japan for critical components and facilities needed for manufacturing high-tech products.[41] Caught in the uneasy limbo between the technology-rich advanced countries and the labor-intensive manufacturers of the less developed world, Korea's attempt to move up has not gone unnoticed by the technological powers-that-be. Firms in Japan, the United States and Europe, on the alert for possible depredations by their Korean rivals, have become extremely cagey about giving them any technology, except at exorbitant prices. Some foreign firms have started pulling the rug from under the Koreans. Kyocera, a Japanese company, for instance, faced with the loss of its Korean market for a component used in fax machines—a Korean company was ready to market the same item—lowered its price drastically, effectively sealing out its would-be domestic rival.[42] The Korean success in 4 mega byte (MB) and 16MB DRAMS may well have been a flash in the pan, one unlikely to recur in any other industry. The Koreans have also lagged behind in developing strategic alliances domestically, while the country's technological xenophobia and the perceived threat to firms in advanced economies make the formation of international alliances including Korean firms an unlikely eventuality. The fact that the Korean *chaebol* are widely diversified further complicates Korea's technological future. Given the plethora of industries in which they compete, determining the areas to which they will channel their limited (by advanced-country standards) resources becomes a vexatious issue. The *chaebols'* move into Europe, North America and parts of their home continent has aroused a ferocious clamor for market reciprocity—a demand that the Koreans are finding irrefutable. Result: more funds needed for defending domestic markets and even less for R&D. Korea's stated ambition of raising R&D spending to 5% of GDP may therefore be both vainglorious and counterproductive.

Taiwan offers us a study in even more government involvement in science and engineering. In an economy dominated by small and medium enterprises (SMEs), the government *must* act to ensure that technological sustenance is provided for and that the economy of the future is being created even as today's successes are being played out. SMEs operate closer to the survival margin than their larger cousins do, while their agility and flexibility make for somewhat less resistance to new ideas, even if they originate elsewhere. The Industrial Technology Research Institute (ITRI) is the apex body responsible for keeping the nation's R&D ahead of, or at least abreast with, the best in the world.[43] ITRI has a full-time staff of over 6,000, of whom nearly 10% have doctoral degrees. It is not a coordinator but a performer of R&D in fields as varied as chemicals and optoelectronics, computers and pollution control and advanced materials and space research. It undertakes contract work from SMEs, and, in fact, one-third of its $45 million budget is funded by its client firms. If a particular innovation was funded by a specific firm, the idea or product is handed over on a nonexclusive basis; that is, anyone can adopt it and use it. Naturally, this causes some grief among the firms concerned. When the idea needs more work, it again imposes a burden on the firms most interested, since their R&D budgets might not support the investment needed. ITRI has also nurtured the formation of strategic alliances to enable firms to pool their know-how and budgets to compete against increasingly wary foreign competitors. With a view to shortening product development times, consortia headed by Acer and by Tatung came together and successfully launched personal computers (PCs) in a little over a year—considerably less than they used to take before. Alliances have also included foreign partners such as Sun Microsystem, IBM and Intel. ITRI's ability to spin off ventures has helped Taiwan build capabilities in fields like semiconductor manufacturing and specialty steels. Firms in these industries are guided and often run by present and past ITRI officials. Again, as in the case of Korea and even Japan, much of the seed technology used in ITRI came from abroad, either through collaboration with RCA, Phillips or other firms/research institutes abroad or through researchers returning after obtaining advanced degrees abroad (primarily the United States). A word about China. The country's rulers are only too aware that technological weakness will only prolong China's subservience to the West and its relatively advanced Asian neighbors. The communist regime got a rude awakening in the early 1990s, when the Gulf War revealed the technological weaponry (both literally and fig-uratively) arrayed against it and other less developed countries. Incentives are being offered for foreign firms to invest in China, the pot being partic-ularly sweetened if the multinational holds out the promise of introducing new technology into the country. The most attractive technologies have strong linkages to other industries, too. Automobile manufacturing and aircraft manufacturing are two such industries, and the government is bending over backward to inveigle firms like GM, Toyota, Boeing and Air-bus into, in a manner of speaking, its parlor. How about China's indige-nous research and development capabilities? Some capabilities exist, no doubt, but as much needs to be undone as done.[44] Most research facilities, for instance, are parts of government institutions whose goals may have little relationship to market needs. About 1,000 research institutes super-vised by the Chinese Academy of Sciences and various ministries possess the bulk of the material, facilities and human resources needed to conduct R&D. Even among the large and medium enterprises (apart from the af-filiates of MNEs) over two-thirds do not undertake any R&D. The town and village enterprises (TVEs) formed through private initiatives at the local level possess considerable initiative and drive but lack the resources or the technical ability to make more than marginal changes in products.[45] China's technological future is clouded with uncertainty in spite of the fact that MNEs are setting up shop there in record numbers, many in techno-logically advanced industries. Aware of the fact that only their technology separates them from their vendors and alliance partners in China, foreign firms do not transfer all the know-how needed for countries like China to strike out on their own. Even worse, as skill levels rise, MNEs can always do what they did in Malaysia—introduce greater automation into produc-tion, which lowers employment while making the product's design and manufacturing process even more opaque.

The predominant position the United States enjoys in science and tech-nology is reinforced by the number of articles contributed by American authors to scientific and engineering journals. U.S. authorship was one-third of the more than 400,000 articles published, while, astonishingly, half of all internationally authored pieces had at least one American contribu-tor.[46] In a clear indication that universities are trying to bridge the gap that often exists between basic research and product development, academic institutions are applying for patents more frequently than ever before. (Three percent of all patents awarded in 1994 were to these institutions, triple that of a little over ten years earlier.)

A significant pointer to a country's ability to undertake and keep pur-suing an intense R&D regimen is its educational system, particularly ad-vanced education in science and engineering. The United States has been a proven front-runner in this regard and continues to excel. For instance, the number of doctoral degrees awarded increased from 18,000 to 25,000 between 1985 and 1993. Most of the increase was attributable to foreign-born graduates (10% of all academics in science/engineering in the United States are Asian), of whom nearly one-third stay on in the United States for at least a year after graduation. Of the 20% who receive one-year postdoctoral appointments, a fair percentage stay on indefinitely in tenure-track positions. Certainly, the United States has educated a large comple-ment of scientists and engineers who are working, or will work, in Asian countries—Taiwan, South Korea, Japan, India, China and so on—which will undoubtedly enrich their native lands' technological futures. However, while here, they undoubtedly serve to deepen and strengthen this country's foundation and superstructure in a range of technological endeavors. Japan, interestingly, has increasingly attracted foreign doctoral students, so much so that in 1993, 40% of doctoral students in technical subjects were from abroad, including over 1,000 students form China. Moreover, the Japanese have started modeling their curriculum and mission more along the Amer-ican pattern.[47] That is, rather than serve as a "finishing school" for industry by instilling and cultivating applied skills, universities are providing can-didates with the depth of knowledge and methodological rigor that will enable them to conceptualize problems and refine experimental skills. True, most Asian countries score far higher than the United States in tests of scientific knowledge. (In one recent instance, Singapore scored the highest in both math and science.) But scientific research is not conducted by high school students. Without an educational system that can support diverse interests and an intensity of inquiry, organizations willing to fund an ac-tivity that may bear little or tremendous fruit and a government with a firm belief in the importance of science and pockets deep enough to act on this faith, science and technology will either founder or have to be artifi-cially sustained on borrowed vitality.

Curiosity and a willingness to take on the unknown drove the explorers of the fifteenth and sixteenth centuries to find out what lay beyond their direct realms of experience. Balboa, Vespucci, da Gama and Columbus certainly were not averse to hunt for vast treasures or convert various peo-ples to what they viewed as the one true faith. But curiosity lay at the core of their efforts. The early scientists, too, were urged onward by a desire to know why eclipses occurred, why certain stars were not visible at certain times of the year, why light seemed to bend when it entered water and so on. They combined this natural curiosity with a system of observation and measurement, which either supported or refuted their theories. Later, as gadgets and devices became commonplace, the application of science to technology proceeded apace. The desire to reach into the unknown, how-ever, is also at the heart of any technological civilization, and countries that can foster creativity and the spirit of inquiry will do best at building a symbiosis between science and technology that will nurture and enable self-sustaining growth in both. All others must depend on external assistance to keep their science and technology moving forward. While much of science consists of "big science" conducted at large universities and/or corporations in teams that consist of scores of members, span continents and have budgets running into millions, if not billions, of dollars, the constant search for better explanations and a deeper understanding of phenomena and the ability to use these answers to better serve humanity are what the technological enterprise is all about. Whether it be the development of Proscar (a drug to treat enlarged prostate) by Merck, the videocassette player by Ampex, the personal computer by Apple or xerography by the Haloid Corporation, creativity, dissatisfaction with current explanations and an urge to improve upon the status quo go hand in hand with market forces in driving the scientific process ceaselessly and inexhaustibly. The pull of the marketplace and the push of imitating the West are strong within Asian companies and countries. On whether the flame so essential to provide the energy and illumination for the path ahead, does, in fact, burn in Asia, the conclusion is clear: not even Japan can lay claim, so to speak, to being the continent's Prometheus.

NOTES

1. John McPhee, *The Control of Nature* (New York: Farrar, Straus and Giroux, 1989).

2. The desire to understand nature through science serves to clearly distinguish sixteenth- and seventeenth-century Europe from the Islamic, Chinese and Indian civilizations of that era. True, Europe's fragmentation gave rise to the operation of (almost) free markets, but that in itself was hardly sufficient to set European civilization apart or to progressively improve the economic lot of its population. Paul Kennedy in *The Rise and Fall of the Great Powers* (New York: Vintage, 1987) capably summarizes the driving forces behind Europe's ascent (pp. 3–30).

3. The dependence of scientists and technologists on validation of their work by the market is evident in basic and applied R&D performed in corporations like Procter & Gamble and Merck. Robert Waterman provides interesting vignettes of how market-technology-science interfaces are managed in *What America Does Right* (New York: Plume, 1994), pp. 197–204, 209–27. While large firms like Bell Labs, Dow Chemicals and IBM have been in the forefront of maintaining the flow of ideas among science, technology and management, entrepreneurs in areas such as biotechnology and information systems are constantly expanding the envelopes of science and technology with commercial intent.

4. As Thomas Kuhn points out ("The Essential Tension: Tradition and Innovation in Scientific Research," in C. W. Taylor (ed.), *The Third University of Utah Research Conference on the Identification of Scientific Talent* [Salt Lake City: University of Utah Press, 1959]), scientists are rigorously grounded in "normal" science. They do not commence their education with innovative or unconventional ideas but, rather, acquire a thorough knowledge of the prevailing paradigms (pp. 162–74). Later in their careers, of course, while collaborating with others on teams of researchers ("big science") funded by the government and/or industry, pursuing

directed research as corporate scientists and so on, the purpose of scientific effort does take on a pragmatic sheen. However, to paraphrase Kuhn, paradigm shifts arise essentially because of discontinuities and a failure to fit observation to explanation, not because they will find favor with the marketplace.

5. Daniel Boorstin in *The Discoverers* (New York: Random House, 1983) observes that inventions like the clock became novelties at the court with little, if any, impact or demand among the public at large—a far cry from the time consciousness and organization that the introduction of clocks induced in Europe. The inability to manufacture devices like clocks in quantities sufficient to satisfy a mass market further impeded the flowering of technology in the Middle Kingdom (pp. 56–72).

6. Capitalism has often been described as a system that breeds inequity, the owners of capital becoming richer, with labor growing relatively indigent. See, for instance, Robert Heilbroner, *The Nature and Logic of Capitalism* (New York: W. W. Norton, 1985), pp. 42–46. The income disparity apparently endemic to capitalism notwithstanding, the fact that people have become wealthier on average, enjoying healthier lives and so on speaks to the beneficial effects of capitalistic systems on the population considered in its totality.

7. Boorstin, *The Discoverers*, pp. 116–20.

8. Ibid., pp. 150–64.

9. Though there is some truth to the argument that Europeans searched for a sea passage to India in order to get their hands on that land's spices (for an entertaining elaboration on this thesis see Salman Rushdie, *The Moor's Last Sigh* [New York: Pantheon, 1995]), Columbus, Vespucci, Balboa, da Gama and Magellan (and their royal funders) expended vast quantities of money, time and effort on exploration in the hope of recouping material and spiritual returns. Boorstin, *The Discoverers*, pp. 235–66, provides a persuasive synopsis of this thesis.

10. Rushdie, *The Moor's Last Sigh*, pp. 186–94.

11. Michael Adas, *Machines as the Measure of Men* (Ithaca, N.Y.: Cornell University Press, 1989), pp. 79–82.

12. Ibid., pp. 89–95, 177–89. Unfavorable comparisons between Europe and China during the nineteenth century were made by numerous writers, most of whom dismissed the Chinese as being incapable of breaking free of their past or of independently developing technologies and scientific thought. The atrophy of creativity and a reluctance to learn from abroad were seen as characteristics of Chinese civilization.

13. As Adas observes, James Mill's disdain for Indian achievements through the ages and for its state of development around the beginning of the nineteenth century shaped English and perhaps Western public opinion at that time. Mill's uniformly low opinion of Indian society, religion, law and art was in accord with his contempt for Indian achievements in science (ibid., pp. 166–72). Though prejudice may have colored Mill's rather extreme statements, his perspective on Indian capabilities to pursue independent ventures in "rational" fields of knowledge merits consideration.

14. Dalhousie's attempts to break the hold of Brahminic tradition in India included the use of technology, for example, railways, to stimulate new activities and patterns of thought by breaking away from the stranglehold of the past. A sense of fulfilling a "civilizing mission" reached its culmination in India during Dalhousie's tenure as governor-general (ibid., pp. 225–27).

15. Boorstin, *The Discoverers*, pp. 73–77.

16. Nature, as an entity to be "objectively" studied, understood and ultimately controlled, was a distinctively European perspective, one that was clearly distinct from viewing nature as part of oneself, as inscrutable or unknowable (Adas, *Machines as the Measure of Men*, pp. 210–18).

17. Karl Popper, *The Logic of Scientific Discovery* (New York: Basic Books, 1989). In testing theories, Popper has argued that a positive decision supports the theory only temporarily or until it is falsified. In fact, Popper defines a scientific theory as one that can be refuted by experience (pp. 35–41).

18. Kuhn, "The Essential Tension," p. 235.

19. Michael Dobbs-Higginson, *Asia Pacific: Its Role in the Coming World Disorder* (London: Mandarin, 1994), pp. 42–45.

20. As indicated earlier, Daniel Okimoto's *Between MITI and the Market* (Stanford, Calif.: Stanford University Press, 1989) is as close to a classic as one can get in its comprehensive and intensive insights into the workings of this powerful Japanese agency. MITI's willingness to allow imports and to encourage licensing of technology is detailed in this work (pp. 25–28).

21. Yoko Ishikura and Michael Porter, *Canon Inc.: Worldwide Copier Strategy* (Boston: Harvard Business School Press, 1983).

22. See, for instance, Taiichi Ohno, *Toyota Production System: Beyond Large Scale Production* (Cambridge, Mass.: Productivity Press, 1988).

23. Though there are shelves upon library shelves of books devoted to TQM, one of the better conceptual expositions linking Japanese practice to American theory may be found in Richard Schonberger, *Building a Chain of Customers* (New York: Free Press, 1990).

24. The R&D ratio (R&D spending as a proportion of GDP) appears to have gradually drifted downward in the United States and Germany, while shifting marginally upward in Japan (*National Science Board, Science and Engineering Indicators, 1996* [Washington, D.C.: U.S. Government Printing Office, 1996, NSB 96-21], pp. 4-36, 37).

25. Actually, the United States spent more on R&D in 1993 than its four closest rival nations—Japan, Germany, France and the United Kingdom—combined. However, the nondefense R&D ratios of Japan and Germany (2.7 and 2.4% respectively) were significantly larger than the 2% spent by the United States (ibid., p. 4-38).

26. Ibid., p. 4-36.

27. Ibid., p. 4-41.

28. Ibid., p. A156.

29. Ibid., pp. 6-23, 24.

30. Edwin Reischauer, *The Japanese* (Cambridge: Belknap Press of Harvard University Press, 1977), pp. 225–27.

31. Scott Callon, *Divided Sun* (Stanford, Calif.: Stanford University Press, 1995). Callon punctures the balloon of MITI's infallibility in picking winner industries and the myth of corporate cooperation in Japan in pursuit of the common good. Unaware of what lay ahead, MITI floundered, and distrust prevailed between Japan's mighty firms.

32. Ibid.

33. *National Science Board*, p. 4-43.

34. Hedrick Smith, *Rethinking America* (New York: Random House, 1995), pp. 360–63.

35. *National Science Board*, p. 4-45.

36. Ibid., pp. 6–11.

37. Fumio Kodama, "The Emerging Technological Trajectory of the Pacific Rim: Concepts, Evidences, and New Schemes," in Denis Fred Simon (ed.), *The Emerging Technological Trajectory of the Pacific Rim* (Armonk, N.Y.: M. E. Sharpe, 1994), pp. 28–53.

38. Ibid.

39. In information systems, the Japanese have had a successful track record in notebook and laptop computers. However, apart from this set of products, they have performed dismally in networking. Firms like Fujitsu and NEC missed connections with the burgeoning market for PCs, Local Area Networks (LANs) and LANservers. They are big on parts and peripherals but no-shows in providing system solutions (Francis McInerney and Sean White, *Beating Japan* [New York: Truman Talley, 1993], pp. 34–43).

40. Whether it be to invest directly in R&D or indirectly through the promotion of research institutes/collaboration, the government has played a major role in the funding and performance of R&D in newly prosperous nations like South Korea and Taiwan. See David O'Connor, "Technology and Industrial Development in the Asian NIEs: Past Performance and Future Prospects," in Simon, *The Emerging Technological Trajectory of the Pacific Rim*, pp. 69–72.

41. "Korea's High Technology Strategy," in Simon, *The Emerging Technological Trajectory of the Pacific Rim*, pp. 85–91.

42. Ibid., p. 98.

43. David O'Connor, "Technology and Industrial Development in the Asian NIEs," in Simon, *The Emerging Technological Trajectory of the Pacific Rim*, pp. 69–72.

44. Zhou Yuan, "Reform and Restructuring of China's Science and Technology Systems," in Simon, *The Emerging Technological Trajectory of the Pacific Rim*, pp. 213–38.

45. Jingping Ding, "Technological Transformation and Renovation in PRC Industry," in Simon, *The Emerging Technological Trajectory of the Pacific Rim*, pp. 242–43.

46. *National Science Board*, pp. 5-33–36.

47. *National Science Board*, p. 2-20.

5

The Creaking
Asian Organization

Openness and accessibility are the hallmarks of science, not in the sense that its tenets are within the grasp of everyone but in the sense that anyone who wishes to challenge an observation, method or finding is free to do so, provided one does so in an open, accessible way. There is no aristocracy in science save that of knowledge and no high priesthood except for those who have mastered their areas of specialization. In principle, even a neophyte can challenge a recognized authority, provided there is sufficient evidence to overturn the prevailing wisdom. Within its portals, therefore, science is a democracy, where outcomes are decided based not on a plurality of votes but on the weight of knowledge, reasoning and data adduced in support of the competing candidate theories. Science is a democracy of ideas that has, until now, flourished best in functioning democracies. The exceptions have been Nazi Germany and the Soviet Union, and the exceptions, as always, prove the rule. Both fascists and communists have achieved success of a sort in orchestrating the national science effort in pursuit of national goals. Hitler's Germany tolerated little dissent and, in fact, actively persecuted a Jewish minority with considerable scientific talents. A narrowly focused scientific effort—mainly directed to serve military purposes or enhance the glory of the fatherland—was a characteristic of both Germany and the Soviet Union under their respective totalitarian regimes. True, Japan, South Korea, Taiwan, Malaysia, Indonesia and the other countries in East and Southeast Asia have made remarkable economic strides in recent years, and it would be absolutely graceless and unrealistic to deny their economic achievements. But are the roots of growth deep and well dispersed? If one of the foundations for durable growth, the kind of growth that will enable gaining on today's advanced countries, is a healthy, self-sustaining scientific research system, Asia has far to go. The democratizing effect of science—its openness and accessibility—was complemented by a similar impact achieved by technology. The latter, however, was, and is, more direct in its influence on us in our daily lives. The great engineers and inventors of our time and through the ages have never been ivory tower dwellers, lost in fascinating worlds and problems perhaps of no interest or immediate relevance to anyone else. Business savvy and entrepreneurial skills have gone hand in hand with technical abilities. Thomas Edison, Henry Ford, Cyrus McCormick, Steve Jobs, Walt Disney, Fred Smith, Ken Iverson and Bill Gates are a representative sample drawn from the long list of successful technical entrepreneurs. These technological adventurers were just as much explorers as were Columbus, da Gama, Glenn or Armstrong. While the latter explored, and continue to explore, our physical environs, the inventor-businessperson plumbs the extent and nature of human needs or even creates them. Edison's invention of the incandescent lamp, for instance, was not driven by a clearly articulated need, but it undoubtedly generated tremendous pent-up demand once its benefits became widely known. Edison, with little formal education, was ever the practical man of ideas.[1] He knew little classroom science but knew how to put science to work for him. He is credited with being the first to establish an industrial laboratory, a facility to conduct applied research and developmental work. Edison's 1,093 patents and his success at getting his own corporation off the ground (we know it as General Electric) speak to his ability to span the gap between science and the marketplace. Few have been as talented as Edison in giving substance to the abstract or in the range of their creative foraging. Ford's efforts were more focused.[2] He was far more a manager than engineer, implementing the standardization techniques made famous by Whitney to lower his costs of manufacture. He was perceptive enough to realize that, in the absence of purchasing power among the buying public, his cars would remain unsold. Raising the minimum wage to a then outrageously high five dollars per day was not an act of altruism (a trait he would have disavowed strenuously) but one of survival. Ford was no inventor, having put the automobile together from numerous borrowed ideas, but he was unquestionably the first to bring the car, economically and logistically, within the reach of anyone who earned a reasonable wage. The automobile has had a remarkable social impact on the United States and, indeed, on any society in which it has become pervasive. A willingness to move to new locations, a desire for independence and increased distances from one's place of work to one's home are some of the marks of an "automobile society," and Ford, surely, did not anticipate or intend all of these repercussions. But Ford's drive to make an affordable vehicle has changed our attitudes and behavior, as well as our economic policies. Every country entertaining any ambitions of becoming an economic power must establish its own automobile industry because of its numerous technological linkages—to steel, parts manufacture, plastics and glass production and so on.

Cyrus McCormick was more of an inventor than was Ford but showed some of the latter's flair for marketing his product.[3] Finding it difficult to convince farmers of the superiority of his reaper, McCormick took to the road, demonstrating to his skeptical audiences how great his product truly was. When he found that potential buyers could not afford his invention—which, as one might expect, was the result of adapting existing concepts to his needs—he instituted the practice of installment purchases so his customers did not have to pony up a forbidding amount to start with. On finding that he was unable to meet his delivery commitments, McCormick decentralized his operations so his facilities would be nearer to his centers of demand. What Ford and McCormick did for their creations, Charles Merrill did for something he did *not* invent[4]—stock ownership. Initially devised as a way to generate more resources by tapping a wider financial base, which, incidentally, served to separate ownership from management in publicly owned companies, shares were, well into the twentieth century, concentrated in a few institutional/corporate hands. Merrill, based on his experience selling retail stocks, decided that mass merchandising was the wave of the future. He saw no reason why equity ownership should be any different. It was just a matter of time, advertising and the establishment of retail outlets before his vision became a reality: Americans were buying goods and ownership in the firms that made them in larger numbers than ever before. Disney, unlike Merrill, did not just reconfigure an industry—he gave birth to it. Not only did he create cartoon characters the public took to readily, but he brought them to the screen through animation, a medium and art form that sprang from his own genius and fertile imagination.[5] Parlaying this novel art form into commercial success and translating his vision of hands-on entertainment for the child in all of us into the reality of theme parks were integral to making Disney's magic a part of our everyday lives. Fred Smith, the founder of Federal Express, built a multibillion-dollar company around the simple idea that there was a huge demand for overnight parcel delivery and facilitated implementation of his concept by setting up the hub-and-spoke system used by airlines and by pioneering retailers like Wal-Mart.[6] Systems to measure performance in minute detail, to reward success, to ensure career development options and so on have helped Federal Express expand its operations even in the face of widespread imitation. Steven Jobs could have done with a less sincere form of flattery from IBM and numerous other competitors and knockdown suppliers who whittled away Apple's initial advantage gained by putting massive computing capabilities within the reach of anyone who so desired. "User-friendly" became the watchword of the personal computer industry—another instance of technology being democratized by an eager, active management. Bill Gates carried the egalitarian distribution of processing power even further by applying Apple's "windows" approach to the operating system he designed for IBM machines.[7] How he then managed to make Big Blue dependent on him—just as tugboats exercise control over mammoth supertankers—is the stuff legends are made of. Ken Iverson of Nucor (a producer of steel in so-called minimills, which are not so "mini" anymore, some of them with capacities of around 1 million tons a year) did not create a new product.[8] Steel had been a successful industry, feeding the demand activities in all advanced countries. While the American steel industry rested on its laurels in the 1960s and 1970s, the Japanese struck hard at it by establishing gigantic steel mills to garner economies of scale and low costs, particularly for export markets. The American steel minimills flourished in the teeth of Japanese price competition by using scrap metal, which was available in plenty, melted and processed in electric arc furnaces. The technology for doing this was relatively unproven, and Iverson took a tremendous risk by investing nearly $500 million in a mill near Crawfordsville, Indiana, for implementing a hitherto untried German design for making thin slabs in a continuous process. Iverson was not the inventor of the process, nor did he risk his own money. The willingness to take the risk on an untested concept and the will to make the idea work have been, and are, however, critical to the continued well-being of American capitalism.

The Japanese, too, have had their share of entrepreneurial leaders who took their firms to industry leadership. Konosuke Matsushita and Soichiro Honda, who founded their eponymous companies, and Sony's Akio Morita come readily to mind. Certainly, their mercurial temperaments enabled them to see their firms through the difficult initial years and to set in place systems to serve them efficiently in their maturity. However, each of these (and other) remarkable men was refining ideas from the West. Honda developed his own designs for small engines based on the motorcycle engines extant at the time. Matsushita's success in televisions and VCRs was rooted firmly in manufacturing efficiencies, standardized formats and marketing effectiveness, while Sony adapted the use of semiconductors to miniaturizing electronic equipment and became increasingly venturesome—more so than its larger cousin, Matsushita—by developing products like the Betamax VCR format, high-resolution televisions, digital audiotapes and so on. It may be noted that even the marketing success of the *kaisha*, or the large Japanese firm, was based on principles developed abroad, primarily the United States. "The consumer is king" became a watchword in the 1980s for the Japanese sensitivity to the marketplace, and a customer obsession is obvious on the part of all Japanese firms. Anyone who has been requested to fill out a postpurchase consumer survey by Toyota or Honda will vouch for the primacy of the customer to the *kaisha*. The almost dogmatic Japanese devotion to market share derives from the prestige it confers in public perception. It is almost impossible for new entrants to succeed against well-established competitors. Stories of meteoric rises like those of Microsoft, Federal Express or Southwest Airlines are highly unlikely in a Japanese context.[9] The entrenched firms fight newcomers for sales tooth and nail, even if in related industries with the potential to affect them down the road. The shiver that the possibility of "excess competition" and its consequent shakeout sends down Japanese spines is a cold one indeed. Change in market positions, if it occurs at all, is glacial, which is no surprise in a land where traditions are so highly valued and defended. The desire to bring better and more affordable products and services to the marketplace burns no less bright in the corporate soul of the *kaisha* than it does in the most customer-conscious American or European firm (assuming, that is, that corporations *have* souls). However, woe betide the firm that tries to rock the boat by taking on the reigning market-share heavyweights. Indeed, this resistance to changes in the pecking order is one of the less surmountable obstacles to the entry of firms from other countries—they, too, are newcomers to the market, irrespective of their size, capability or reputation. Just ask Kodak, Motorola and Toys "R" Us. The Japanese, nevertheless, were no trailblazers in marketing. Their postwar drubbing in foreign markets when they attempted to export cameras and toys taught them a valuable lesson, one they put to good use soon thereafter. When Deming and Juran instructed Japan's managers in the nuances of statistical quality control, the seed, to use a biblical metaphor, fell on fertile ground.[10] Just as the Japanese had been eager to absorb "hard" technology from abroad from the late nineteenth century onward, they were a receptive audience when the gurus of quality visited and revisited Japan. True, as is their wont, the Japanese listened, adopted, experimented, modified and improved. Their vision of total quality management bore no more than a passing resemblance to the word as preached to them by their American mentors. Starting with statistical methods, the Japanese gradually built a system of management practice that emphasized satisfaction of customers' needs, employee involvement and an unremitting search for improvement. The customer orientation was not a hard sell to Japanese salarymen and to the rank and file, since the importance of market share to the perceived success and prestige of the firm was unquestioned, and customers were obviously critical to the building of market share. The detailed work that the *kaisha* embarked upon to substantiate their commitment to customer satisfaction is impressive indeed.[11] Techniques such as quality function development and customer satisfaction surveys helped them better understand and serve external customers, while the use of process flowcharts and cause-effect analysis improved service to internal customers (i.e., employees whose task performance depends on inputs from their colleagues). Just as customer satisfaction as a concept was borrowed from the United States and refined in Japan, the notion of employee involvement had been extensively studied in England and the United States. Researchers in sociotechnical systems, for instance, had concluded, well before the Japanese assault on world markets began, that teams given relative autonomy in carrying out their work develop techniques and mechanisms to maximize efficiency and the utilization of full potential of group members.[12] The Japanese took to group-based techniques and management a little more easily than did their counterparts in the West, partly because of their intrinsic need to seek affirmation from their colleagues, their desire to conform and a craving for harmony at any price. The loss of face that poor team performance would entail is too abhorrent to contemplate. Peer pressure and the iron grasp of hierarchy help teams function effectively, not because of mutual respect but because organizational and national aspirations will not have it any other way. Neither regard for their colleagues nor reverence for their organization motivates the salarymen to subordinate their personal needs and private lives to the common good. Fear of losing face and of public embarrassment, a punctilious regard for status and the tenacious desire to maintain or enhance corporate reputation (typically in the form of market share) energize the Japanese managerial class.

This does not, by any means, imply that employee involvement in Japan is a sham. Both salarymen and line workers have collaborated over the years to successfully implement diverse, group-based participatory practices. Quality circles, cross-functional teams, "natural" work teams and design review teams, as well as the co-optation of suppliers/customers on one or more of such teams, have not only taken team-based organization to new levels but also served as models for previously skeptical workers, managers and top executives in other parts of the world.[13] I do not intend to question or cavil at the real achievements of the *kaisha* in enlisting employees in the implementation of strategies and in quality deployment. The motivation underlying the high level of involvement is, however, not altruism but conformism. When Japanese firms assert, with pride and confidence, that they do not believe in organizational charts, that they trust their employees enough to flatten their organizations and expand managers' span of control, that groups are empowered to make decisions and so forth, they are not telling us the whole story.[14] They omit to mention that their people possess a finely tuned sense of hierarchy, assessing status distinctions with great precision, that certain decision criteria (dealing differently with insiders than with outsiders, framing situations within a given context etc.) are commonly shared and that no employee would question or contest any management action or belief. Japanese employees do not, therefore, participate extensively and intensively because they want to but because they *have to*.

One of the pillars on which TQM rests is that of continuous improvement, a "natural" for the *kaisha*.[15] The relative importance attached to process over results indicates that improvements in *how* tasks are performed matter more than the outcomes themselves. Goals, particularly cor-

porate-level ones like market share, are given their due importance, and
the fight to maintain a company's standing in the marketplace is an unremitting one. But departmental, sectional and individual goals are often dif-
fuse and vague, intentionally so, because employees are expected to do their
very best, even going beyond the call of duty—since "duty" is, on purpose,
undefined, the striving can be endless—to achieve goals that are perceived,
often dimly, to beckon them forward. Under these conditions, it may seem
unlikely that implicit goals can motivate employees to do more—until we
recall that peer pressure, the fear of embarrassment and a desire to conform
hold the salaryman in a tight embrace. He becomes a prisoner of process.[16]
No detail is too small for teams to painstakingly analyze and improve. Is
cycle time too long? Perhaps identifying times consumed in operations,
waiting, storage and movement will help us reduce time wasted in non-
operational activity. Still not satisfied? Benchmarking our process against
our competitors should give us pointers on areas for improvement. Too
much time taken up in pilot production and market rollout of new products? Involving manufacturing and marketing in the design process might
ameliorate or eliminate these problems. Clearly, under a process-heavy system, performance appraisal (PA) must also be process-driven, which means
that criteria for evaluation are likely to be as open to interpretation as the
goals themselves. PA systems in the *kaisha* do not belie these expectations.[17]
Employees are assessed, moreover, without being told the basis for the
assessment or the details of the evaluation written by their superiors. The
secretive nature of the assessment process and the lack of feedback give
one the general feeling that one is shooting at moving targets with a rather
erratic gun in a darkened room. All is made clear ten years after induction
into the firm, when the lights are turned on, and the best performers are
revealed. Till the decade elapses, however, keep trying your best, and things
will work out!

Total quality management fits snugly with Japanese corporate practices
that favor a lack of clarity, value the means over the ends, view customers
as the most important stakeholders, discourage rocking the boat, shun giving offense, have an intuitive grasp of relative status and a myriad other
behavioral nuances—some of which would be anathema to firms elsewhere,
particularly in the United States or Europe. They would, in fact, be anathema to Japanese employees as well if the mechanisms for enforcement—
ostracism, shame, embarrassment for the family—were not so dire, rigid
and immediate. One of the most widely shared images of the Japanese
manager is that he or she—nearly always a "he," so I shall dispense with
the use of gender-inclusive language forthwith—has a long-term vision, sees
the big picture and always has the interests of the entire firm at heart.
Certain contextual conditions in Japan have helped shape and reinforce
this impression. Banks have, in the past, made low-interest, long-term loans
to large firms, making the latter less sensitive to immediate returns. Stock-

holders have been passive onlookers, taking what they are given in the form of dividends and price operations. Companies make major investments in plant and equipment—Fuji, Nippon Steel, Toyota, for instance—to service demand for the next decade or so. Employees, especially in the larger firms, generally stick with the employer who hired them straight out of college until they retire. Firms, in their turn, do not, as a rule, "downsize" or "rightsize" at the slightest sign of a dip in sales. Rather, they do their utmost not to lay off anyone for any reason whatsoever. All of this clearly points to the strategic nature of corporate and managerial outlooks. Right? In this, as in most other aspects of Japan, things are not what they seem. Dispel, if you can, the popular myth of the sagacious, inscrutable Orient, a misconception that was carried to Europe and, later, America by overly romantic scholars overcome by the "wisdom of the East." People who have few material possessions can afford to be spiritual; they have not yet seen the dawn of materialism, the hope of wealth. Ascribing to civilizations the same traits they once possessed in their glorious, yet penurious, past is not only naive but also dangerous because it implicitly assumes they will do things they are incapable of. Conjuring up visions of Suzaki or Hideyoshi when one does business with, or competes against, the *kaisha* undoubtedly makes the encounter more exotic but adds little of information value.

Take MITI's purportedly farseeing ideas and policies. VLSI, as we saw in an earlier chapter, was a successful venture in its outcome, though the distrust displayed among the participants in the consortium was not a happy omen. The reluctance to share information doomed later projects like the supercomputer and fifth-generation efforts, both boldly conceived, both designed to preempt likely actions by leading foreign competitors, both relative shots in the dark (with no footsteps to follow). MITI, moreover, bet on the wrong technological horses (gallium arsenide memories, Josephson functions for switching), which took the entire research in the wrong direction. The success that was claimed at the end was no more than a duplicitous effort to save face. But, from MITI's perspective, it is as important to hedge your bets as it is to win. Later, MITI decided to boldly go where no one had dared to go before. With its usual percipience and aplomb it decided to coordinate the building of an airplane that could fly five times as fast as sound.[18] MITI also felt driven to announce a plan to develop micromachines capable of traveling through arteries. Given the threadbare funding provided by MITI and the reluctance of Japanese firms to invest in long shots, the prospects for success are bleak. If, however, a Western firm or agency were to actually develop these products, MITI would declare that its crystal ball was right on target. If the firms had only executed their assigned roles properly, Japanese talents and resourcefulness would have triumphed again!

The *kaisha* themselves are no more visionary in their thinking or strategic in their actions than their erstwhile guide, philosopher and friend, MITI.

When Sony decided to acquire CBS Records and Columbia Studios, it was aching to get back at Matsushita for snatching the VCR market away from it.[19] Sony rationalized its strategy in an attempt to combine the hardware and the software of entertainment. Fearing a Sony end run around it, Matsushita decided to acquire MCA, also ostensibly for its "software." Both firms were credited with vision and insight, qualities their Western rivals were said to be lacking. Today, after the passage of many years and the loss of many hundreds of millions of dollars, the decisions can be seen for what they were: myopic actions by cash-rich corporations trying to steal a march on their competitors, while painting grandiose pictures for their publics. The Daiwa securities scandal (and others like it) and the numerous Japanese real estate investments in Japan, the United States and other parts of the world—clinched admittedly during periods of yen appreciation— also fit this pattern of short-term actions couched in long-term language.

The fact that Japanese firms have succeeded so brilliantly as exporters and more recently as manufacturers and marketers abroad cannot be attributed solely to their management system, as some scholars have done. Rather, a combination of circumstances, some intended and others fortuitous, converged to make the Japanese rise a reality. Governmental support, initial low wage levels, targeting of industries, collaboration between firms, technology licensing and adoption, foreign competitors' passivity, employee docility, centralized operations and the absence of Asian rivals at home were among the factors that started, and have kept, Japan moving forward. Some of these factors, as we have seen earlier, have been eroded or have vanished (e.g., low wage rates and a lack of Asian competition), while others are no longer the motive forces they once were (interfirm cooperation and government help). Still others are gradually evolving into forces whose impact is beginning to be felt; for example, employees are no longer as submissive as they were soon after the war, while the need to decentralize operations worldwide has meant trouble for the Japanese MNC. Adjustments are being attempted, but the jury is still out on how effectively Japanese firms can function abroad on a continuing basis. Some may sing the company song—both literally and figuratively—only if the beliefs expressed and language were changed, while others may not take too easily to singing the company song in the first place. Making accommodation to diversity, not a strong suit with the Japanese, will increasingly test and puzzle them in the years to come.[20]

The label "Made in Japan" is a welcome sight to most consumers anywhere in the world, particularly for automobiles, cameras, audio and video systems, electronic games and associated product lines. However, this label is an increasingly rare sight today. Labor is expensive in Japan, forcing forms to invest in manufacturing centers like Malaysia, Indonesia, China and Thailand. Tit-for-tat protectionism has reared its none-too-handsome head in the United States (e.g., the so-called voluntary restraints on exports in the auto industry) and in the EC in the form of local content laws, making it difficult for the Japanese to export directly from their shores to nations that consider them antagonists. For all the talk of globalization and positive-sum games, nations, as we have seen, guard their perceived endowments and rights aggressively when backed into a corner. The Japanese, pragmatic as ever, have found ways to insinuate themselves through all the cracks and loopholes afforded them. Denied entry as Japanese-made products, the latter now enter advanced countries' markets incognito. Factories in countries like Malaysia, Thailand and China export to the United States and Europe goods made with Japanese know-how, equipment and frequently with key, expensive components imported from Japan.[21] The situation may be likened to a masquerade ball where no one can be denied admittance because his or her true identity cannot be disclosed. Of course, if only residents can participate, other avenues must be explored, and you can be sure the Japanese have researched all possible options in great detail. Joint ventures, technology alliances and foreign direct investment have all been tried with a view to gain footholds in countries that do not take kindly to the job insecurity arising from peripatetic manufacturing. While the Japanese ventures in the United States are well known (the GM–Toyota joint venture in California, Toyota's factory in Kentucky, Nissan's in Tennessee, the Sony plant in California, etc.), there are numerous plants in Europe as well.

The decision to invest in facilities abroad is an expensive one. In addition to the obvious, relatively tangible costs like the purchase of land, new equipment, transportation, etc., there are hidden costs. Among the less obvious costs are training of labor to enhance skills, of expatriate managers to adjust to local conditions and of local managers to adjust to new styles, creating a cadre of reliable, responsive suppliers, suffering the possible loss of shared technology and the potential erosion of employment at home. The Japanese *keiretsu* is a form of networked and/or conglomerate organization that has sprung up, like the legendary Hydra, in spectacular fashion to replace the original conglomerates (*zaibatsu*) banned during the Occupation.[22] Hitachi, Mitsubishi and Sumitomo are widely diversified firms, yet not in such dissimilar industries that their constituent firms cannot do business with one another. Products made in one division can, and often do, draw upon the expertise and production/service capabilities of their siblings in the *keiretsu* family. Typically, this makes it difficult or even impossible for new firms (foreign or local) to buy from divisions that supply to their fellow divisions. In addition to the market share obsession shared by most Japanese firms, *keiretsus* serve as a further impediment to entry into industries. The difference is that the defense of market share is visceral, and the *keiretsu* barrier is structural. Another manifestation of the *keiretsu* phenomenon is when relatively undiversified firms, focused on an industry (e.g., Toyota, Honda, Nissan), develop a group, more often an army, of dedicated suppliers. As long as the retinue stayed within Japan, the only problem created by them was the impossibility, for a new firm, of enlisting any of these existing suppliers to their service. The leading firms in the world automobile industry have, therefore, remained no more than bit players in Japan. When conditions—protectionism, need for foreign technology—dictated that they manufacture cars in their most lucrative markets, the Japanese displayed what I have earlier termed the "Dracula syndrome." There is no intention or desire on my part to ascribe vampirish tendencies to the *kaisha*, though firms in the United States and Europe that have accused the Japanese of predatory practices might argue that companies from the Land of the Rising Sun often *do* go for the jugular. The reluctance to step out of familiar environs could prove to be a continuing and crippling handicap for firms that lay claim to be corporate citizens of the world.

On the surface, it appears that many Japanese firms are minimally vertically integrated. The automobile industry, for instance, is said to be heavily dependent on outsourcing, with around 80% of the final value of a car comprising components purchased from suppliers, as opposed to no more than 50% for American car companies.[23] The ratios for other industries, though considerably lower, still convey the impression that Japanese firms are market-driven in their operations, unlike their control-freak Western counterparts. That is, rather than rely on corporate control to keep internal part and system suppliers on track, the Japanese prefer to trust their (outside) suppliers to achieve their customer satisfaction goals. Again, the reality is quite different from the perception. The Japanese would have us believe that their unique approach to customer–supplier relationships gives them the best of both worlds—the choice of the marketplace and the bonds of organizational membership. However, the interorganizational ties are formed typically from a base of common ownership. Mitsubishi, for instance, has a mutual stockholding ratio (among *keiretsu* members) approaching 30%, though the Mitsubishi Bank held about 60% of the shares of the entire group. The mutual ownership ratios are slightly lower (17% and 24%, respectively) for Mitsui and Sumitomo, the next two largest *keiretsus*.[24] The three other *keiretsus* have compatible ratios. The collaboration among group members is formal. The Presidents' Club in each *keiretsu*, consisting of the presidents of the various firms' divisions, meets on a regular basis to keep the connections among the constituent elements of the alliance strong and current. By no means are the members of the vertical/horizontal groupings compelled to do business with one another. Loyalties, however, do run deep, and the tendency to stick with internal suppliers is as powerful as one would expect in a fraternal, quasi-market system. The more focused companies known as *shitaukes*, which include Toyota and Honda, whose connections are vertical, are obviously bound even more strongly together.[25] The development of JIT manufacturing in the automobile industry was facilitated by the fact that the buying firm (e.g., Toyota) owned shares in major vendors. There was, unquestionably, a commitment to Toyota on the part of its supplier to deliver quality goods when and in the quantities needed. But it certainly doesn't hurt a firm's bargaining position to own part equity in another organization that needs its business. In addition to owning equity in one another, *keiretsu* members also depute executives to serve as directors on each other's boards. The assignment is commonly done on an asymmetric basis, with banks getting the lion's share of directorships and firms at the downstream position of the value chain (i.e., manufacturers and assemblers of final products) sending more representatives to serve on upstream boards than vice versa. Equity, directorial, financial and other dependencies create a tight network of relationships and obligations. Relationships serve the long-term needs of organizations since the past serves as a guide to, and indicator of, the future. But if a relationship turns into a commitment regardless of the conditions or consequences, trouble can ensue, particularly if there are better choices available outside the range of intrafirm options. True, *keiretsu* members are not always required to buy/sell to one another, but the compulsions of the insider/outsider dichotomy, so insidious and strong in relationship-oriented societies, ends up favoring an internal exchange rather than a market transaction, even where the economies dictate otherwise. Of particular interest here are the vertically integrated *shitauke* like Toyota, Honda and Nissan. Being accustomed to controlling most or all of their supply chain at home, they are, in a manner of speaking, genetically predisposed to dealing with familiar faces, with suppliers who have a feel for the mutual, yet asymmetric, dependency they have thrived on in the past. Wherever these firms establish operations, they attempt to carry their "native soil" as accompanied baggage. Obviously, this has great potential for irritating the host nation, which might have laid out an expensive red carpet (in subsidies and tax holidays) to tempt the foreign investor to choose that location. Suppliers bring their own technology, resulting in few technology linkages and improvements in the local economy. Profits accrue mainly to the Japanese MNE and its suppliers (which may be at least partly owned by the parent firm), resulting in foreign shareholders' reaping the lion's share of the rewards. Additional employment will, no doubt, be generated, but considering the high price paid up front for the privilege of attracting Japanese investment, the cost per job (which may be as high as $500,000 in the United States) to the state could turn out to be excessive and difficult to justify. The *keiretsu/shitauke* system carries within it the potential for its own decline both at home and abroad. *Keiretsus*, by keeping a finger in many different pies, run the risk of being spread too thin both technologically and market-wise. Mitsubishi, Sumitomo and Hitachi cover industries as wide-ranging as heavy machinery, electrical equipment, automobiles, electronics and, potentially, aircraft, running the risk of doing none of them exceptionally well. Technological synergies and a customer focus become notoriously elusive and play second fiddle to internal relationships in such firms. Toyotaism, on the other hand, is risky in exactly the reverse sense: all the eggs are in one basket. Unless the Japanese market becomes less restrictive as specific industries go into a tailspin, however, the *keiretsu* and *shitauke* do not face the imminent prospect of cracking under the weight of their rigidities at home. The dangers abroad are more serious and difficult to remedy.

Trusting the known and the familiar is an all-too-human trait, but the Japanese in particular and most Asian societies in general have made a shibboleth out of it. Not only is the Dracula syndrome alive and well, but the Japanese are as exclusionary toward gaijin employees as they are toward unfamiliar vendors. Left with no choice but to hire locally, the Toyotas and the Hondas have, in the past, been quite ham-handed in their human resource practices.[26] Stung by a spate of lawsuits charging discrimination on the basis of gender and race, harassment and so on, companies like Honda have resolved to turn over a new leaf in their dealings with local personnel. However, being accustomed to enterprise unions, conformist employees and cooperative governments, the *kaisha* do not travel well. Their fervent belief in centralization and frequent—in some cases, daily—consultations with Japan does not inspire confidence in their ability to respond quickly to emerging challenges. The *tatemae*, or appearance of local executives having the authority to make decisions versus the reality of headquarters executives being the true power center, is often galling to high-level managers, particularly in the advanced countries. Executive disillusionment, to be sure, is not sufficient to bring the Japanese company crashing down, but slow reactions to changing environments can. R&D, a function that many firms—with great fanfare—declared they had decentralized to their various international operations, is a case in point. The reluctance to trust foreign employees to change product designs, processes, materials and so on still grips Japanese firms like Matsushita, Nissan and Mitsubishi. While the most commonly cited reason to locate abroad in the first place is market access, the tight grip in which market responsiveness through R&D is held by headquarters belies this motivation.[27] The ability to learn from customers seems to be a talent the Japanese have left behind them—or perhaps their unwillingness to trust foreign employees overpowers their desire to be market-responsive. The innovative shortcomings of the Japanese when coupled with the reluctance to delegate R&D decisions to subsidiaries make for a less than propitious technological future. Conformism, hierarchism and incrementalism are the core characteristics of Japanese management, again, ideal properties to launch pursuit from, not the stuff of which pioneering organizations or societies are made. Both strategically and behaviorally, the *kaisha*'s deficiencies will continue to accentuate the national inability to strike out in bold new directions.

Figure 5.1
Information and Societal Frameworks

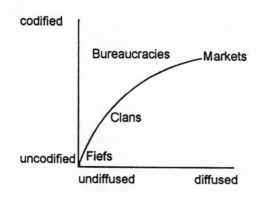

Compared to the *kaisha*, the Korean *chaebol*, the Chinese family business (CFB), the public sector enterprise (PSE), whether Chinese, Taiwanese, Indian or any other, the Indian family business (IFB) or business indigenous to any of the other countries of Asia possess limited capabilities to compete, particularly in foreign markets, and to develop new technologies in their own. Rooted in societies far more familistic than the Japanese (more on this in Chapter 6), the Koreans, Chinese and Indians are better described as fiefdoms based on blood ties. Boisol and Child's framework for classifying societies and their organizations according to the way information is processed is instructive in comparing the diversity of organizational forms found in Asia.[28] Boisol and Child argue that information available for conducting transactions may be codified/uncodified depending on the clarity of rules for processing it, and access to information (and the ability to use it) may range from being widely available (diffused) to closely held (undiffused).

Modernization occurs as societies and the transactions occurring within them move in a northeasterly direction in Figure 5.1, progressing from fiefdoms to market organizations. Most Asian organizations are at the early stages of evolution, with personalistic and relational management predominating. Japanese firms, for instance, with their avowed preference for organizational and personal networking, are, in the main, clannish (e.g., the more tightly bound *keiretsu*) or bureaucratic (firms like Matsushita and Fujitsu), with a fair sprinkling trying to graduate to pure, market-focused information processing (Honda, Toshiba). If Japanese firms eschew corporatist and personalistic criteria in decision making, they will be able to challenge Western firms in the latter's home territories across a broad range of industries. The unwillingness to listen to, and use, information urging them to decentralize and, where necessary, break traditional ties holds them back from becoming the fearsome competitors they could be. The road ahead for the Koreans, Chinese and Indians is far rockier. Organizations native to all three societies are concentrated around the lower left of Figure 5.1, comprising personal fiefdoms, where family connections matter more than ability, personal favors and business affairs commingle freely and the rules governing economic transactions are opaque—or worse, invisible—to all but a select few.

The Korean *chaebol* are striving to break free of their feudal chains, as evidenced by their manufacturing investments in Europe, China and India. Samsung, Lucky-Goldstar, Hyundai and Daewoo have committed hundreds of millions of dollars, funds garnered from their export earnings, to their foreign operations to gain access to markets with great potential for growth and/or likely to become protectionist. The *chaebol* have shown a willingness to invest heavily in R&D as well, with a view to challenging world leaders in industries such as semiconductors, automobiles and large appliances. The results have been uneven. In semiconductors, it appeared for a while that the Koreans had the measure of the Japanese, the Americans and the Europeans but discovered that fearful rivals can turn fearsome. Intel, TI, NEC, Toshiba and Phillips invested ever more heavily, formed alliances where needed, lowered prices, focused on high-end products and so forth, making it amply clear to Samsung, the fledgling Taiwanese firms, the wannabe Malaysians and any others with similar ambitions of gate-crashing the semiconductor bash that industries of the future were not going to be as easy to crack as those of the past. While the *chaebol* do, indeed, have deep pockets, their ability to consistently develop expertise in the high-tech areas they have targeted remains in doubt. Even the size of their caches of money shrinks when viewed in context: the total R&D spending of South Korea is rivaled by that of the world's largest firms.[29] No matter how fast R&D spending grows—some reports indicate that Korea intends to spend more than 3% of GDP on R&D by the year 2000—the limitations of starting from a small base cannot be quickly surmounted. Moreover, the easy credit terms typically extended to the *chaebol* that contributed to make them antagonists to be reckoned with—relatively unchallenged at home and flashy spenders abroad—are coming back to haunt lender and borrower alike. The stop-and-go nature of the economy in recent years does not allow as much governmental generosity as it used to, and some of the *chaebol*, even with the limited foreign firms being allowed under duress to enter the country, are beginning to run into lean times, some folding completely. In the absence of a strategic focus, a core of competence to give them a sense of direction and an understanding of where their technological and market destinies lie, the *chaebol* are condemned to a future of being mammoth, inchoate masses whose least-effective flanks will decay, leaving them with diversified holdings, shrunk but no more effective than they are now. Alternatively, if they voluntarily divest themselves of "noncore" businesses, they will have to modify, radically in certain ways, their management philosophy and practices. For instance, the sparseness of vertical linkages in all their multiple businesses means that the *chaebol* cannot count on a core of dedicated suppliers and retail channels to facilitate their movement to more specialized positions in select industries.[30] Long-term commitments between firms are scare, and, given the heterogeneity of expertise within firms, developing capabilities in-house does not seem likely to happen anytime soon. The owner/family control exercised in even the largest of the conglomerates, the temporal nature of the commitment made to the employee, the personalization of management and middle management's relative impotence do not bode well for the *chaebol* in their bid to take on their Japanese, European and American rivals. They *must*, if they are to succeed abroad, adopt some of the features of their pioneering rivals but, in so doing, lose some of the competitive advantages that got them where they are now.

The Chinese family business (CFB), seen in its various reincarnations and mutations in Hong Kong, Singapore, most of Southeast Asia and, more recently, in the land of its origin, southern China, is far more personalistic than the *chaebol*, which, to begin with, were conceived as diversified, complex organizations.[31] Most CFBs, even the largest like the Salim and Lippo groups of Indonesia, are tightly run by the founder and his close family.[32] Typically, the CFBs are wary of expansion beyond their ability to monitor all their operations closely and in person. While connections between CFBs do exist, they are typically channeled through the owner, making task-based exchanges and transactions difficult to achieve. For instance, dependence on multiple suppliers to feed an assembly operation would become unwieldy to manage if the only points of interfirm contact were the heads of the firms concerned. Vertical integration is unlikely, since that would require monitoring an extended chain of activities. Complex manufacturing activities have, therefore, been beyond the purview of the CFB. They have tended to excel in real estate investments and speculation, retail sales and, in general, any service or manufacturing activities that do not require the management of anything more than the simplest of interdependencies. Activities involving sequential (or serial), reciprocal and interactive interdependencies among firms have generally been given a wide berth by the CFBs and their networks.[33] The archetypal CFBs evolved in Taiwan, where they have remained small in size and scope, except for the likes of Formosa Plastics and Acer. Given the inability of the CFB to grow beyond a certain size, the government of Taiwan has had to establish state-owned enterprises (SOEs) in heavy industry (chemicals, electrical machinery) to ensure that the infrastructural support for economic expansion was available. Personal trust is an intimate part of the Chinese organization, and it exists typically only between members of the same family. The definition of an outsider is even more stringent than in the *kaisha*, where, at the very least, everyone else in the same section or division, perhaps even in the same firm, is an insider. In the CFB, nonfamily employees are outsiders. The patriarch jealously guards his monopoly over decision making, and even the closest relatives are often no more than apprentice managers-in-waiting. The exceptions are the conglomerates (e.g., in Indonesia), where the close relatives who head the various divisions exercise limited autonomy, and those CFBs where scions and heirs, having earned degrees abroad, are allowed some leeway in managing the business, though full autonomy is generally anathema to the founder until he sees an immediate need for a successor to be anointed. Research and development by its very nature is risky, provides uncertain returns and requires depth of knowledge and commitment to an industry. For these reasons, the CFBs are light on R&D, meaning that the state (as in Taiwan) or foreign enterprises (Singapore, Malaysia and Thailand) will have to introduce and upgrade the technologies on which continued employment and growth can be founded. Hong Kong, which prides itself on having negligible state funding for industry, was also not a high-tech haven for foreign firms. Its technological base is minimal, and its reputation entirely derives from the financial expertise it houses. It is not just in R&D that state support has served to stimulate the growth of the CFB. In countries like Indonesia and Thailand, where political maneuvering and finagling can do wonders for a business's future health, the CFBs have demonstrated their ability to win favor with the ruling elite, junta or cabal. Whether to ensure the success of a business run by the president's daughter, to arrange for an expenses-paid education abroad for the prime minister's son or to contribute to the party's war chest, the CFB has never been found wanting where generosity and influence peddling are called for. In fact, habits acquired in Asia seem to follow agents of the CFB across the globe. Recent revelations about foreign contributions to the Clinton campaign by representatives of the Lippo group of Indonesia and by owners of Taiwanese businesses seeking to gain favor among the satraps in Beijing by swaying American policies, if not public opinion, toward the Chinese regime have caused a furor in the United States.[34] Obviously, CFBs, accustomed to co-opting, if not capturing, governments in the countries of the Chinese diaspora, feel they can export their skills at behind-the-scenes manipulation just as freely as they export their products. The *guanxi* web (of relationships and obligations) that enfolds Chinese societies is a great medium of communication and of cementing a network of commitments, but its effectiveness outside its natural environs is dubious, at best.[35] Just as the family-centered, paternally authoritarian, simply structured and minimally integrated CFB seems to be in dire need of redesign, so, too, is the cocoon of *guanxi* likely to increasingly apply the brakes to the forward movement of Chinese-dependent economies and of China itself. One may laud the value of the Chinese handshake—indeed, trust is critical to all business dealings—and the highly personal nature of this approach to managing, but to build a modern economic system of institutions and organization based on the principles of transparency and predictability, the nature of the Chinese business organization must change. The minority Chinese who often came together because they hailed from the same parts of China (e.g., Hokkien or Teochiu) and/or because they were being persecuted in their adoptive homeland, are now the economic cream of their societies.[36] Any enhancements of their contributions to output are likely to come not from increases in inputs or by discovering further niches to exploit but by developing new capabilities, entering new industries and expanding the horizons of trust beyond the immediate family. Greater China, that is, the Chinese populations beyond the mother country's shores, generates an economic output of over a trillion dollars, which could, in the opinion of many observers, rival that of Japan early in the next century. But the continued success of the Chinese diaspora requires more than networking and cronyism. If they wish to succeed in unfamiliar markets (e.g., Europe, the United States or even Africa), they will have to undergo a transformation far more radical than that required of the Koreans and Japanese.

The Indian family business (IFB) is similar to the CFB in its style, decision locus and government relations.[37] One major difference is that some of the IFBs have grown to mammoth proportions due, in part, to competing in protected markets, an emphasis on import substitution, quotas on production resulting in high prices and so forth. Successive Indian governments, in seeking to avoid MNE domination of the economy, ended up facilitating the growth—perhaps bloating might be a better word—of the most ambitious and rent-seeking IFBs. The houses of Birla, Tata, Modi and Ambani (the last better known as Reliance Industries) fed from the government-replenished trough and achieved near monopolistic positions in their chosen lines of business—a conclusion the government had assiduously sought to avoid by barring by the entry of MNEs.

One of the legacies bequeathed by the British when they departed India in 1947 was the managing agency system.[38] Dominant shareholders would appoint professional managers to run the firm according to their dictates. These managing agents often ran many companies and, as agency theory would suggest, pursued their own objectives, which were often in conflict with those of individual firms or their shareholders. A by-product of the managing agency system was that a cadre of professional managers (many of them Indian) acceded to positions of authority after independence. Since then, a growing interest in, and appreciation for, management as a profession have led to the establishment of numerous institutions offering graduate degrees in management, formal techniques in management are widely practiced and even family businesses have taken to dispatching individuals likely to assume power to business schools (at home or abroad) to acquire the skills necessary to assume their positions of authority. When all is said and done, however, even the largest IFBs have made heavy weather of competing against MNEs that have recently entered the Indian market. Decades of complacency, corruption and corporate inbreeding have created behemoths too inflexible and technologically backward to hold their own against the world's best.[39]

Both China and India, in keeping with their ideological bent at the time, invested large amounts of government money in setting up public sector enterprises or PSEs (India) and state-owned enterprises or SOEs (China). In China, these enterprises were in keeping with the state's ownership of all the means of production, while in India they were meant to prevent privately owned monopolies in vital sectors. In both countries, they became inefficient laws unto themselves, technologically backward and no more than social arms of the state. In India, the PSEs succeeded in throttling the private sector wherever the two overlapped, thereby damaging the economy doubly. Both countries are trying to shrink government ownership of firms at present through privatization and by making them compete for resources and customers. However, closing them down is not a viable option because of the labor unrest that it is likely to unleash. Paradoxically, public ownership in both countries was one of the bulwarks against the familistic business practices traditional to much of Asia. The shrinking of the PSEs/SOEs is likely to result in a reversion to management based on "know-who" rather than "know-how," a retrogression neither country can afford. Ironically, one of the few rays of hope for both India and China in the managerial arena is that foreign MNEs will, in addition to investing capital and technology in the two countries, leave a permanent mark in terms of transmission of management skills on a large scale. The dissemination of knowledge through the numerous institutes offering business degrees (even if some are of the fly-by-night variety) indicates a surging interest in management as an avocation. But how well the techniques and methods of rational organization withstand the onslaughts of nepotism, cronyism and other entrenched traits and ways of life is yet to be seen. The prognosis, based on information thus far available, is not an optimistic one. The family-based businesses will continue with their personalistic or quasi-personalistic methods until forced to face MNEs in open competition, at which time they will capitulate, unless governments come to their rescue. The MNEs will continue to be islands of rationality in an ocean of favoritism.

In closing, a paradox: the highly nationalistic countries of Asia must increasingly adopt Western management ideas but, in so doing, become less indigenous in their approach to issues and decisions. The more they cling to their traditional ways of running businesses, the longer they remain incapable of competing with Western firms (at home and abroad) and of nurturing the development of technology.

NOTES

1. Jonathan Hughes, *The Vital Few* (New York: Oxford University Press, 1986), pp. 158–66. Edison was fairly successful in business, too, attracting, unlike Whitney, who depended on government money, considerable private financing for his ventures. The wizard of Menlo Park formed one of the first known research teams, though he ran them with an iron hand. They were far from cooperative, egalitarian groups.

2. Ibid., pp. 282–96.

3. Harold Livesay, *American Made* (Boston: Little, Brown, 1979), pp. 53–84.

4. Daniel Grass, *Greatest Business Studies of All Time* (New York: John Wiley, 1996), pp. 91–105.

5. Ibid., pp. 123–41.

6. Ibid., pp. 267–83.

7. Ibid., pp. 335–51.

8. John Savage, "Nucor's Keys to Quality Approaches," in Y. K. Shetty and Vernon Buehler (eds.), *Productivity and Quality through People* (Westport, Conn.: Quorum Books, 1985), pp. 237–52.

9. Noboru Yoshimura and Philip Anderson, *Inside the Kaisha: Demystifying Japanese Business Behavior* (Boston: Harvard Business School Press, 1997), pp. 104–14.

10. See, for instance, Mary Walton, *Deming Management at Work* (New York: G. P. Putnam & Sons, 1980).

11. These and other techniques of quality management are covered in detail in Masaaki Imai, *Kaizen* (New York: McGraw-Hill, 1986) and Shigeoi Shingo, *Zero Quality Control: Source Inspection and the Poka-Yoke System* (Cambridge, Mass.: Productivity Press, 1986).

12. E. L. Trist and K. W. Bamforth, "Some Social and Psychological Consequences of the Longwall Method of Coal Gettings," *Human Relations* 4 (February 1951): 3–38, provide an account of early attempts in the field.

13. Imai, *Kaizen*.

14. Harmony, it is true, is a feature of Japanese organization. That does not mean that trust prevails. For an insider's view of the dysfunctionalities to which the *kaisha* are prone, see Yoshimura and Anderson, *Inside the Kaisha*, pp. 83–90.

15. As Nobaru Yoshimura and Philip Anderson point out, even the very process of recruiting and training the salarymen serves to instill a process orientation (ibid., pp. 22–31). They then learn to accord the highest priority to organizational processes, which is further reinforced by the ambiguity of goals. Vague goals also serve to emphasize the power of managers as well as to stimulate higher levels of effort than if one knew what one was pursuing. Far from anticipating or sensing corporate expectations, therefore, the salaryman may be better envisioned as floundering without a clear sense of what he is supposed to achieve (pp. 160–68).

16. When process is translated as attitude, effort or observance of form, effectiveness could suffer (ibid., pp. 52–54). A mind-numbing repetition of the primacy of process all too easily masks the strictures likely (from one's supporters and peers) for not achieving results. The *kaisha* are not result-blind. Western firms that adopt a process-only orientation could find themselves in trouble very quickly.

17. Ibid., pp. 199–204.

18. Ibid., pp. 150–52.

19. Envy of market share often drives apparently sane chief executive officers (CEOs) in Japan to make strategic moves for no other reason than that their rival has adopted a particular strategy and might steal a march over them. Truly, individual pragmatism can become mass hysteria at the national (e.g., during the Second World War) and corporate (e.g., the Sony–Matsushita strategy of keeping up with the Joneses) levels. Yoshimura and Anderson neatly debunk the myth of the *kaisha*'s rationality while acting out their *Yokonarabi*, or acts of imitative retaliation (ibid., pp. 134–37).

20. Foreigners are obviously "outsiders," making for an uneasy relationship with local employees in the *kaisha*'s operations abroad. Keeping senior American executives in the dark while lower-ranking Japanese employees consult with Tokyo is inconsistent both with a task orientation (generally viewed as the basis on which Western organizations rest) and with a relationship focus (the guiding principle of the Japanese organization). Such actions serve only to erode the *kaisha*'s credibility and viability in a none-too-familiar environment (ibid., pp. 75–78).

21. *Kudoka*, or the hollowing-out process, has hit Japan about two decades after the United States experienced the painful contractions associated with the flight of capital and low-cost manufacturing overseas. Yen appreciation in mid-1985 accelerated the flight of jobs (William Greider, *One World, Ready or Not* [New York: Simon and Schuster, 1997], pp. 69, 80, 252–53). As Thurow points out, in spite of Japanese investments abroad, few countries run surpluses with Japan. For instance, China's surplus of about $20 billion with the United States was almost matched by its deficit with Japan (Lester Thurow, *The Future of Capitalism* [New York: Penguin, 1996], pp. 194–95).

22. Many of the present-day *keiretsus* are grouping in which parts spun off during the dissolution of the *zaibatsus* have been reconstituted into a viable whole. A few of the intermarket groups are alliances of corporations (e.g., Matsushita) (Michael Gerlack, *Alliance Capitalism: The Social Organization of Japanese Business* [Berkeley: University of California Press, 1992], pp. 28–29).

23. Ibid., p. 63.

24. Min Chen, *Asian Management Systems* (London: Routledge, 1995), p. 171.

25. Jeffrey Hart, *Rival Capitalists* (Ithaca, N.Y.: Cornell University Press, 1992), p. 41.

26. Susan Ehrlich and Andrall Pearson, *Honda Motor Company and Honda of America* (Boston: Harvard Business School Press, 1989, pp. 118–39.

27. Francis McInerney and Sean White (*Beating Japan* [New York: Truman Talley, 1993]) advocate "customer co-location" or establishing organizations that can communicate directly with customers. The Japanese have typically been adept at marketing feedback but not quite so nimble at R&D responsiveness. While many *kaisha* have "decentralized" R&D, their Japanese R&D groups tend to dwarf anything they have abroad. For instance, in 1990, Hitachi's labs in Europe and America had 27 employees, while the Japanese R&D groups numbered well over 100 times that number (p. 163)—obviously not an effective way to service the evolving needs of customers abroad.

28. Max Boisot and John Child, "The Institutional Nature of China's Emerging

Economic Order," in David Brown and Robin Porter (eds.), *Management Issues in China* (London: Routledge, 1996), pp. 35–58.

29. David O'Connor, "Technology and Industrial Development," in Denis Fred Simon (ed.), *The Emerging Technological Trajectory of the Pacific Rim* (Armonk, N.Y.: M. E. Sharpe, 1994), p. 91.

30. Richard Whitley, "East Asian Enterprise Structures and the Comparative Analysis of Forms of Business Organizations," *Organization Studies*, 11, No. 1 (1990): 47–74.

31. Whitley (ibid.) describes the CFB as being "embedded in elaborate networks of personal obligation" (p. 59), a far more personalistic web than any that the *chaebol* have woven.

32. Chen, *Asian Management Systems*, pp. 88–93.

33. Whitley, "East Asian Enterprise Structures."

34. The possible infiltration of the Democratic National Committee and, hence, even of policy making in the Clinton administration by individuals with connections to the PRC has caused widespread alarm. Some of this lobbying-through-involvement was also the result of a rivalry between Taiwan and China over winning the favor of an executive branch that looked open to persuasion (*The Wall Street Journal*, April 3, 1997).

35. Chen (*Asian Management Systems*, pp. 52–62) has fascinating insights into the building and operation of the *guanxi* web. Although Chinese often have compartmentalized business and personal relations (e.g., by avoiding business dealings with neighbors), evasion of *guanxi* and of its attendant *renqing*, or social obligations, becomes more difficult in urban, industrial settings. Also, as Chen points out, procedures and rules are more difficult to enforce in *guanxi*-driven organizations.

36. Though present-day CFB owners are not limited to doing business with someone from the same town/province, such was the custom in earlier years. The desire for a defining identity, the sense of loyalty to themselves and to their native China and a refugee-like ambition to make good are articulated fully in Joel Kotkin, *Tribes* (New York: Random House, 1992), pp. 165–86.

37. B. R. Virmani and Sunil Guptan, *Indian Management* (New Delhi: Vision, 1991), pull no punches in their assessment of Indian management style. The personalistic, familial perspective adopted in Indian firms (including the public sector, in which dollops of overspending, mollycoddling of employees and kowtowing to politicians are also tossed in) is traced to the centralization and personality focus characteristic of much of Indian history and religious tradition. Systems of patronage and using the system to one's benefit when one has the power to do so are all part of accepted practice (pp. 184–92).

38. The managing agency system was banned after India became independent but continues to flourish in camouflage as many Indian families disguise their ability to control firms in which they hold minority stakes (ibid., p. 14).

39. Indian firms, rather than take MNCs on directly, preferred to enter into joint ventures with them. Many of these joint ventures are falling apart, however, partly because the MNCs want greater strategic roles and realize they are in a position to dictate terms even to the biggest of the local firms. See, for instance, *Business World*, July 24–August 6, 1996, pp. 54–60.

6

Asian Values—
Intrinsically Superior?

A brainteaser in mathematics posed to me when I was in elementary school went something like this: imagine a frog stuck at the bottom of a well 100 feet deep. On day 1, the frog jumps 50 feet upward, on day 2, 25 feet up and so on, each day scaling half of what it had accomplished the previous day. After how many days will the (apparently superhuman) frog reach the top of the well?

The answer, obviously, is never. The poor amphibian gets closer and tantalizingly ever closer to the top without ever emerging into the open. I reached the answer, as did most of my colleagues, by laboriously adding each day's progress to the previous ones to find that the required sum of 100 was unlikely to be attained. Later, of course, I realized that this was a simple problem in geometric progression. Later, I also wondered why the frog, when it realized what was happening, did not, so to speak, double its efforts or try different ways of launching itself upward. But that is another tale. (Or, then again, perhaps not.)

The argument presented in these pages suggests an analogous trajectory for the diverse Asian efforts to draw level with the advanced countries of the world. I say "diverse" advisedly—as has been pointed out by numerous observers and repeatedly emphasized in these pages, there is no single Asian formula. Each country has, through a process of experimentation and evolution, arrived at its own brand of growth model. Gerschenkron's thesis that the adoption of similar or even identical economic goals does not inexorably result in pursuing them through the same means is well taken.[1] Unquestionably, imitation does occur. Japan has served as trailblazer and reluctant teacher, knowing full well that the example it set would be emulated to its own detriment. As much as anything else, the Japanese gave their fellow Asians a massive dose of hope, if not optimism, that the hitherto dominant Europeans and Americans were not invincible militarily or economically. The enemy could be defeated and, making it even more enjoyable, with its own weapons. No country can, however, be termed a Japanese clone—or a Korean or Taiwanese clone, for that matter, notwithstanding the temptation, difficult for most observers to resist, to jump to conclusions. *The Economist*, for instance, editorialized that the Asian countries that have more recently undertaken economic reforms and other measures to lift themselves up from poverty were following policies earlier adopted by countries in Southeast Asia, particularly Malaysia. The similarity between, say, India, China and the Philippines, on one hand, and Malaysia and Singapore on the other lies in the invitation to foreign investors to enter the countries, bringing their money and knowledge with them. This policy, of course, differs markedly from the Japanese, Korean and Taiwanese closed-market stand vis-à-vis foreign firms. While this no doubt provides a striking resemblance to the path adopted by Malaysia, it is worth noting that a segment of the growth vector chosen by Japan and South Korea (e.g., the use of licensing to transfer and absorb technology, counting on American indulgence toward a cold war ally) could not be employed by latecomers to the development game, a group that includes Malaysia and Indonesia. Similar courses of action are naturally inaccessible to the even more tardy arrivals like China and India, which, unlike some of their predecessors, have huge markets with which to induce MNCs to enter them. Low labor cost is no longer the only criterion for MNC investment. There are, to be sure, models and inspirations among Asian countries. The key success, however, lies not in reusing the same mold but in an astute and interactive process of trial and error.

The variations among the specific strategies formulated and—often doggedly—pursued by the risen and rising in Asia do not, by any means, suggest that they share no common ground. To the contrary, they share the desire to achieve the same degree of wealth and comfort enjoyed by the colonial powers that held sway over much of the continent until well into the twentieth century. Both the desire and the knowledge that the mission is possible have fired the imaginations and pumped up the energy levels of the population at large. From Pakistan and India in the west to China and the Philippines in the east, Asia is bubbling with excitement. Writ large over the past and the destinies of the entire region is, as numerous scholars have unerringly observed and as this book has reiterated, the active interventionist and directorial part played by the state. Without revisiting the arguments developed and issues broached in earlier chapters, it would be no exaggeration to say that the state has been the axis around which Asian capitalism has revolved, and it seems likely to continue in this pivotal role.

If all it took for a country to achieve prosperity was a perspicuous, wise and determined government to steer and hold its course, rapid economic growth might be far more widely distributed than it actually is. The state has been a necessary, but hardly a sufficient, contributor to the ascendant fortunes of the high-performance nations of Asia. Unquestionably, the people, organizations and institutions in the focal countries must be given due credit for their accomplishments. They have garnered their share of the praise as well. Specifically, some of the traits and abilities that have attracted the most admiration, if not adulation (along with the implied or explicitly stated inferences drawn) are:

- The savings rate, which has typically been of the order of 30% or more of GDP, is far greater than the rates prevailing in any Western country.
  Conclusion: Asians are frugal and willing to sacrifice today on the altar of tomorrow. American profligacy is legendary and is clearly exemplified by the irresponsible use of credit cards and, on a larger scale, the runaway budget deficit.

- Education is highly valued all over Asia. Literacy rates verge on 100% in Japan, Korea, Taiwan and Singapore and are rapidly climbing in the rest of developing Asia. Scientific and technological education is most highly cherished. Singapore, for instance, scored at the very top in both science and mathematics in a recent test given to high school students.
  Conclusion: The human capital available (and being created) in Asia is of a superior caliber, and it is likely to keep getting better since Asians are fully aware of how critical education is to building the knowledge-based society. The gap in science and technology with the advanced countries will only keep narrowing.

- The capacity for hard work is limitless, whether one has in mind Japan, Korea, Malaysia or China. The salaryman on whose shoulders Japan rose to superpower status has his equivalent in the executives and entrepreneurs of the entire region. The work ethic in Western countries, on the other hand, is moribund. Labor unrest, inflated salaries for executives, downsizing and just plain laziness have combined to sap the energies of Western civilization.
  Conclusion: Given the will to work and desire to succeed, all of Asia can only keep getting more and more prosperous. As the indulgent and degenerate West gets increasingly demoralized, innate industriousness will make the Eastern star glow ever brighter.

The conclusions are rather bluntly stated but are by no means the opinions of a radical minority. Numerous scholars and experts in Europe and America subscribe to these and similar beliefs, as do many politicians and an increasing segment of the population in Asian countries. There are, of course, caveats that must be considered in tandem with the kinds of inferences just reached that, in effect, weaken them somewhat. *Savings* rates in much of Asia reached astronomical levels partly because people had little they could spend their money on. With the bulk of the production capacity devoted to exports—government incentives assured an export orientation—little emphasis was placed on making consumer goods, which were generally in short supply. As consumption has risen, savings rates have declined, so much so that even in China, the government is concerned over the declining pool of funds available for investment.[2] Moreover, as Ohmae (1995) has pointed out, variations in accounting practices often led to an overstatement of savings rates.[3] *Education* is undoubtedly high, perhaps the highest item on the priority list of all Asians. Whether it is due to the examination system that historically opened the door to administrative jobs in China and Chinese-influenced societies, the "exam hell" that still determines the futures of countless Japanese high schoolers or the universities bequeathed by the British (or modeled after them) whose blandishments an inordinate number of Indians are unable to resist, Asians of all nationalities need no persuasion of the inestimable worth of a good education. A chasm, however, separates wishing from doing. An exchange from Shakespeare's *Henry IV* is apropos here. In response to Glendower's boast that he could "call spirits from the vasty deep," Hotspur concurs but asks, "But will they come when you do call for them?"[4] Countries like China, Indonesia and India (about three-quarters of the continent in population) have a long way to go before they can claim that their people—particularly those living in rural areas—have access to schools and colleges to match those in the United States and Europe. Even Japanese universities often serve as glorified anterooms or holding areas for those awaiting corporate jobs. Korea and Taiwan are valiantly trying to meet the demand for higher education. At the master's level and above, both the quality and capacity are sorely lacking. The watered-down Ph.D.s offered by numerous Indian universities do not lead to any appreciable enhancement of human capital in that country. It should also be mentioned that much of the Asian preoccupation with education is mainly due to extrinsic reasons. That is, education is seen to be a passport to security and wealth—hence, its allure. Knowledge qua knowledge, learning for its *own* sake, is not what Asians generally mean when they say they value education. Rather than being the noble pursuit of an ideal, education is the pragmatic pursuit of wealth via a college degree. Granted, the thirst for learning for its own sake is hardly widespread anywhere else in the world. But for a part of the world that hopes to seriously challenge for world leadership, economically and socially, the educational system must start inculcating more creativity and curiosity. Excelling in rote learning and in the accepted paradigms of normal science produces "clerical" scientists and conservative engineers, not leaders who can strike out in bold new directions.

Some contend that Asians are, by nature, hardworking and that at least some of the success enjoyed by their respective nations over the past half century is attributable to this trait. There is, of course, no disputing the fact that the Japanese, Koreans, Taiwanese and the residents of the two city-states have established an enviable reputation for long hours on the job. The salaryman has spent most of his life in *and* with his firm, epitomizing the dedication and determination one has come to associate with Japan. Owners and their relatives in the Chinese family business are, in the countries of their diaspora, models of industry and achievement, as one would expect of minorities in foreign, often hostile, lands. But this hardly means that a strong work ethic is integral to the value system of all Asians. The jury is still out on the capacity for hard work of the vast majority of Indians, Chinese and Malays (the latter the bulk of the populations of Malaysia and Indonesia, constituting around three-quarters of the population of Asia). Will they, as their standards of living rise, display the same propensity for putting their shoulders to the till as have some of their neighbors and members of far-flung diasporas?[5] (Even Mahathir's much touted "look east policy" has ridden on the backs of the Chinese in the workforce or Chinese-owned businesses. The future looks a lot like the past, since there are 8 times as many Chinese enrolled in science and 15 times as many in engineering programs as there are Malays.[6]) Until this question can be definitively answered, the debate over Asia's work ethic must remain unresolved. It is also worth considering a few related questions. Did the capacity for hard work appear suddenly after the Second World War? Did the trait evolve gradually once people realized their efforts could affect their lives? If so, could we not say that where the ability and desire to work hard exist (e.g., Japan, Korea), they arose due to the availability of Western markets and technology, in short, that the origins of the Asian work ethic lie elsewhere?

The three issues touched on earlier (savings rates, education and work ethic) are dimensions of a wide-ranging debate that has waxed and waned (more the former) on the subject of Asian values. Leaders of certain countries—notably, Mahathir Mohammed, prime minister of Malaysia; Lee Kuan Yew, former prime minister of Singapore and, more recently, Deng Xiao Ping and Jiang Zemin of China—have taken to excoriating the West for a host of perceived sins of commission and omission. The main sources of these (and other) prominent Asians' resentment toward the advanced countries of the West, particularly the United States, stem from a sense of supreme satisfaction with their achievements. They feel that they did it "their way" and that no one has the right to advise them or offer them suggestions on any matter whatsoever. The gravamen of the Asian position is that, having got where they are through the fruit of their own labors, they should be left alone to pursue goals of their choosing that employ means and are based on values most in keeping with indigenous abilities and cultures. Unexceptionable contentions, the discerning reader is likely to remark, and they indubitably are, so far as they go (more on that momentarily). The argument is extended further by the more passionately partisan when they link Asian values to Confucianism and its attendant work ethic. We are now treading on ground that is considerably less solid. To see why, we will take a brief detour through Confucianism.

Acknowledged as an influence, even if not an overpowering one, in China among the peoples of the Chinese diaspora and in countries originally influenced by China, Confucianism is not a religion. It has no gods, places of worship, priests or dogmas. It has been practiced but not advocated or propagated. Its appeal lies not in conjuring up visions of an afterlife— rendered comfortable or otherwise, depending on one's conduct here and now—or by recourse to abstract notions such as the Trinity or reincarnation. Confucianism prescribes codes of behavior. Through actions, it seeks to construct a social system and thence a core of principles. The Japanese, Korean and, indeed, Chinese preference to act and to learn from doing, in a sense, reflects the Confucian spirit. As has been noted repeatedly by scholars, Confucianism is a way of life, a dimension, if not the entire culture, of a group, nation or race. Unlike other belief systems like, say, Roman Catholicism and Islam, the basic practices of Confucianism are invariant across the world. (Catholic beliefs are universal, but the practices may vary, e.g., protocols for kneeling, standing or sitting or for wishing one another peace, the use of indigenous musical instruments by choirs, priests' attire etc.) The essence of Confucianism rests in practices that demonstrate filial piety and reverence for ancestors, the existence and acknowledgement of status differences, the importance of form, protocols and appearances. In spite of the most strenuous and persistent efforts by the communists to lessen its hold in China, Confucianism has held firm. It seems almost to be a part of the genetic code, to be a cultural gene or "meme," as Dawkins puts it.[7] If there is one virtue that Confucianism values above all else, it is stability. Worship of ancestors and abiding by the prescriptions for behavior governing various relationships (father–son, ruler–subject, etc.) place a high degree of emphasis on not rocking the boat, on an unwillingness to break with the past. The individual, locked in a system of relationships, has no choice but to conform, to accept the *duties* imposed on him. There was a strong temptation to end the preceding sentence with "or her," but that would be going against the grain of Confucianism in its pristine form. Women have no part to play in the Confucian scheme of things. The elaborate stipulations regarding relationships do not include mothers, sisters or daughters. It is not surprising that practices such as foot binding and concubinage originated and persisted in societies where male-dominant traditions were deemed to be beyond alteration or refutation. In many of the countries of the Chinese diaspora, women have joined the workforce and are taking on more active roles in the government, corporations and academe. Does this indicate a Confucian reformation? Not in the least. As soon as Western-style business methods yielded returns, Confucianism had to give ground. Rising incomes and the vast potential for prosperity on a scale hitherto never experienced were responsible for the cracks that developed in the monolithic (paleolithic?) edifice of Confucianism. Where women were needed in factories for intricate or delicate assembly work, they volunteered with alacrity, typically with the encouragement of their fathers or husbands. Where there were no male heirs, family businesses were entrusted to daughters and wives. Under the communist dispensation in China, particularly during the more draconian times, women were given party positions and jobs in industry on a equal footing with men. All this happened in spite of Confucianism, not because of it. If Asia—or at least those parts of it with a Confucian heritage—is to continue on its high-performance path, it will have to shed some of the other traditions that have held it in their firm grasp for centuries. Of course, Confucianism is not the prevailing wisdom in all of Asia. Hinduism (mainly in India, though there are significant pockets in Sri Lanka, Malaysia, Thailand and Singapore) and Islam are the other dominant ways in which people construct and view reality. Neither Hindu nor Islamic societies have been in the vanguard of industrialization in Asia. Malaysian and Indonesian affluence is, in the main, attributable to the influx of foreign investment and technology and to the initiative and energy of their Chinese minorities.

What, then, do Asian leaders and others who presume to speak for all of Asia mean when they cite Asian values as the reason for letting them pursue their destinies according to their own lights? A philosophic difference they might have in mind is the centrality consistently accorded to fulfilling one's responsibilities and performing one's *duties*, as opposed to the Lockean liberal tradition in which individual rights are prized above all else—duties to one's parents, to one's immediate family and relatives, to the state.[8] Rather than talk about individual rights exercised independently of others in society, Asians, albeit to varying degrees, are conscious that their existence as a society depends on individuals' sharing their responsibilities to one another. That is, collective well-being can be ensured only by individuals' doing what is ordained by custom and tradition. The superiority of the Asian system, the argument goes, lies in the subjugation of the individual to collective rights and freedoms in order to preserve the integrity and health of society. The success of the whole reflects the success of its parts. Evidence of the beneficial outcomes of actions directed toward collective rights is produced and displayed with great pride. Crimes both violent and otherwise are committed far less frequently per capita in the developing and nearly developed countries than in the United States or much of Western Europe. Murders, rapes and armed robberies are nowhere near the epidemic proportions they have assumed in parts of the developed world. Other indications of social decay in the West are no less depressing. Divorce rates hover around 40%, drug use and drug-related crimes have left few areas in the United States untouched and the education system has been described as inadequate to meet the needs of the twenty-first century. Little wonder that prominent Asians are not impressed with capitalism in its Western liberal form. Why should we jettison a system that works, they say with more than a tinge of smugness, for another whose results are abysmal? Not only has Asia grown in leaps and bounds economically, it has done so with government orchestration. Even more implausibly—almost heretically, from the Western liberal standpoint—it has done so with the curtailment of individual freedoms. Oh, yes, freedoms are not being curtailed—people are merely more responsible and conscious of their duties to one another. Why, argue the votaries of Asian capitalism, should the West not take a leaf from our political books and try a system in which collective rights determine individual responsibilities? Why, indeed?

The perceptive (and patient) reader has, in all likelihood, guessed by now that there is another, less appealing side to Asian capitalism, social achievements and value systems that its ruling politicians would rather not talk about. Take, for instance, the indicators of social vitality and stability. While crime rates are low by American standards, there is increasing lawlessness in China, and in Taiwan and a rise in juvenile crime in Singapore.[9] The wide disparity in incomes between residents of the SEZs like Shenzen and people in central and western China has created an army of unemployed, former agricultural workers, numbering upward of 200 million, on the move, searching for employment. If the SOEs start shedding employees in an effort to become more efficient or as a result of privatization, the transient population could increase, creating serious law and order problems for the government. Taiwan has seen crime assume massive proportions, so much so that leading politicians, including President Lee himself, have to apologize for the brazen nature of the criminal activities—some by people in high places—that have, by and large, gone unpunished.[10] White-collar crime is rampant in South Korea, touching the highest office in the land. When bribery and venality have become commonplace, and honesty is measured by how much one accepts or expects, not by whether or not one is on the take, a society is, indeed, in trouble. The argument that Asians have different societal and value systems looks more and more like an excuse, not a plea for empathy. What does one label the acts of a ruling elite in Indonesia that ruthlessly suppresses dissent and dispenses favors to its minions and cronies?[11] Or the so-called benevolent military officers who have ruled Thailand for much of the past half century and who do not blink an eye when a toy factory burns down, claiming 300 lives?[12] Reason for the fire: no warning prevention or extinguishing equipment. Such niceties cost money, and MNEs (in this instance, a Hong Kong-based firm) might flee if regulated "unduly." India's labyrinthine bureaucracy is fertile ground in which corruption sprouts and grows prolifically. Misuse of authority has numerous variants, many of which augment one another. The Customs Department cooperates with the Narcotics Bureau, which, in turn, is hand in glove with the local police, all united in an unholy alliance with the blessing of top bureaucrats and even heads of government ministries. One reason economic reforms have run into heavy weather in India is that they will tend to reduce the power of bureaucrats and politicians to earn their illicit princely incomes. Judicial activism and a nascent resolve to prosecute crooks no matter how lofty their perch are a welcome attempt to attack the disease. But India will have to do more, much more, to cast off the badge of shame that its top functionaries have pinned on it. Of course, corruption and callousness are not exclusive to South Korea, Indonesia, Thailand and India. They do serve to demonstrate, however, that in the absence of full accountability on the part of public officials, the nature of criminality in developing countries, where free expression is constrained, differs from that in countries where individual liberties are respected and guaranteed.

Other social indicators are not as reassuring as one might expect. South Korea's divorce rate has tripled since 1970, while that in Taiwan and in Singapore has doubled since 1980, Hong Kong's has risen ten times over 20 years and even in China the number of broken marriages increased threefold during the first half of the 1990s.[13] Given the subsidiary role assigned to women in most of Asia, one could be "respectable" and enjoy sexual freedom only if one was male. Sexual mores are changing now. There is far more openness—nudity is allowed in certain public places in Japan, call-in shows are popular in Shanghai and casual sex is no longer taboo in Delhi. Warnings against drug use are routine in the more affluent parts of Asia. Even Singapore, the model state, has become increasingly concerned about the casual and addictive use of drugs among its youth. Increasing prosperity, particularly among the privileged minorities, has apparently given birth to the problems of plenty: ennui and the search for that extra excitement, whether it be the latest "designer" drug, spouse swapping, aphrodisiacs made from tiger whiskers—you name it, and it's probably happening in Asia right now. Make no mistake, most parts of Asia are exciting places to be at the beginning of a new millennium. Certainly, not everything listed earlier is criminal or even illegal. But if these are what define Asian values, a lot needs to change in such a system before it is held up as a model, as something to be proud of.

The one social institution of which Asians of all nationalities are justifiably proud is the family. Not only are parents and children considered an indivisible unit, but grandparents, uncles and aunts, cousins and even more distant relatives look out for one another, even live under the same roof. As anyone who has experienced the vicissitudes of living in an extended family knows, it is neither unalloyed joy nor distress. There is, of course, a built-in support system in the arrangement. Economic assistance in difficult times, counsel on a wide variety of matters and even free baby-sitting services are readily available, often taken for granted. There is a price to be paid for these apparently free services, however. Where the male head rules the household with an iron hand, no one is free to make one's own decisions, whether these be career-related or personal, major or trivial, and irrespective of whether one is financially independent or not. Privacy in such households is defined by its complete absence. Yet there is something comforting and protective in being under this sort of family umbrella. As sociologists have observed in societies where primogeniture (i.e., property devolving solely to the male heir) is not the custom, all the sons remain on the ancestral land since they share the family wealth equally. In such societies, it has been argued, industrialization takes longer to gain momentum since there is less incentive for property owners to relocate in search of, or after finding, employment. Japan and most of Western Europe, where primogeniture has been the rule, have found a ready source of labor in the younger siblings who had no incentive to continue living on the family property if they could find well-paid jobs elsewhere.[14]

In his well-reasoned and insightful book *Trust*, Francis Fukuyama points out that the immediate family is such a strong binding force in China and among the Chinese diaspora, in Korea and even in southern Italy (to which list I would add India) that other societal institutions seem weak and even transitory by comparison.[15] Whereas, for instance, adopted children are accorded the same rights and respect as biological ones in Japan, they have no legal or social standing in China or Korea. A preoccupation with blood ties creates, according to Fukuyama, an inability and a reluctance to enter into close, instrumental relationships with anyone who is not an immediate relative. The proliferation of small, family-owned businesses, networks connecting families and conglomerates whose divisions are headed by family members in countries like Taiwan, Hong Kong and Singapore, as well as among the Chinese minority in the other countries of the region, is proof of this thesis. Since the family is the only unit to which individuals feel a sense of belonging, the only viable organizations are those that are centered around the family. In Taiwan, which was among the earliest of the Chinese-based societies to achieve economic recognition, the vast preponderance of firms are small businesses, with only a few large enough to compete internationally (e.g., Formosa Plastics and Acer). Though the small CFBs do have nonkin employees, the latter have little say in the running of the business and are generally interested in moving on so they can start their own concerns. Since owners typically expect to exercise detailed control over the businesses, growth is restricted and is often resisted, unless there are trustworthy, close relatives who are capable of making their own decisions. The Indonesian conglomerates like the Lippo and Salim groups are just overgrown family businesses, each division of which is managed by the founder's children or their spouses. Since the president of the country shares the family-first philosophy, the CFBs and the ruling elite in Indonesia have been involved in a durable, mutually beneficial partnership. There are numerous large family businesses in India as well. Multidivisional firms like those owned by the Birlas, Tata, Ambanis and others have grown by deputing family members to head important business segments, by making full use of a sheltered market and by getting favored treatment from the government, which, until 1991, strictly regulated most industries. The government, as in Taiwan, had to step in and make mammoth investments in petrochemicals, heavy electricals, shipbuilding and steel. Korea might appear to be an exception to the rule that in family-focused societies, large businesses are a rarity. The *chaebol*, after all, are not family-owned, and they *are* huge. But if we look closer, we find that the *chaebol*, too, have members of the founding family in positions of authority. In many cases, a single extended family owns a controlling interest.[16] To complete the story, the Korean government generously subsidized and supported the *chaebol* in their early years. Funds were, moreover, made available on easy terms with loans backed by the government. (Some of these "sweetheart deals" are now coming back to haunt the banks concerned. It turns out that not all the *chaebol* made wise investments. A few banks have collapsed.)

Despite the commonly shared perception that the United States is a highly individualistic society, Fukuyama posits that there is a strong communitarian streak in American society that draws people to membership in church groups, public service organizations, neighborhood associations, school-related activities and so forth. The rugged frontier spirit and the culture of social Darwinism are not a myth but appear to coexist with philanthropy and communitarianism. In that sense, the United States and Japan bear a stronger similarity to each other than does the United States to, say, southern Italy or Japan to China or Korea.[17]

Large business organizations occur "naturally" through evolutionary growth in their Japanese and American habitats but have to be artificially created and/or propped up in most Asian countries. On the face of it, this conclusion seems to be of no more than academic interest, a piece of almost irrelevant trivia. After all, even if Taiwan and Korea are culturally not programmed to create and manage large organizations, it does not seem to have adversely affected them. Their rise and that of China thus far do not reflect the existence of any handicap or impediment to improving their economic performance. However, when a society's organizations are limited to sizes appropriate for family control, and the degree of trust reposed in anyone beyond the immediate family is minimal, *the state* steps in to create what no one else will. The state's role in such societies runs not just to the formation of SOEs/PSEs (as in China and India) or to lavish subsidies and favors to large, privately owned businesses (as in Korea and Indonesia) but also to compensate for the absence of institutions necessary to bridge the gap between the family and the state, between the intimacy of a small group and the impersonality of the nation. The tendency in family-dominated societies is to jealously guard the rights and privileges of the small group, ignoring those of everyone else. As Fukuyama observes, common resources such as the physical environment often get rapidly eroded because the guiding principle of such societies is that one should do everything to maximize a family's prosperity even if it reduces the viability of the rest of society.[18] The state must therefore intervene to ensure that, to use management phraseology, "suboptimization" does not occur, detracting from the optimum performance of the whole. The environmental degradation that has occurred in Asia over the past quarter century perfectly illustrates the point. Deforestation, strip mining and pollution of various types have combined to create a nightmarish scenario in much of Asia. Family-owned businesses have done part of the damage (especially in Taiwan and Korea), but the PSEs/SOEs share some of the blame as well (particularly in India, China and Taiwan), while MNEs must shoulder a significant portion of the blame. Where governments are hell-bent on industrialization, and families do not see the societal forest, so to speak, for the monetary trees, the nation as a whole pays the price.[19] The tragedy of the commons could strike often and hard where communitarianism is a scarce commodity, unless facilitative and safeguarding mechanisms are created—indeed, imposed—by the government.

Low "social capital" societies, therefore, may achieve economic growth but are dependent on the government to create a sense of nationhood, to bridge the gaps between families, to establish impersonal institutions for legal redress, to extend credit without bias, to improve the lot of minorities and so on. The state has a wide-ranging social role to play that, when considered in the light of its prominent economic role, makes it an even more dominant player on the Asian stage. It is not surprising that many of the statist, noncommunitarian societies of Asia are also lacking in individual liberties. In countries where kinship determines the amicability or hostility of one's attitude and behavior toward others, the state becomes an invaluable arbiter, a buffer of first and last resort. It is as though the people themselves proclaim, Save us from ourselves, for we most certainly cannot. When leaders loftily assert that *their* people share different values and must not be judged by Western standards, they are correct but not in the way they intend. Their implication is that individual (human) rights are an alien concept and that Asians are dutiful and disciplined. Wrong. Noncommunitarian Asians are narrowly focused on a small kinship group, not on the rest of their nation or society, much less other Asians or the rest of the world. Accepting the need for individual rights would require that the bonds (chains?) of the family be broken first. Until that is done, much of Asia (barring Japan) will remain incapable of forming wider associations, of throwing off the shackles of the state, of conceding that human rights are not a Western artifact.

There is also a strong temptation among Asian cognoscenti to equate liberty and democracy with chaos and indirection, particularly in less developed countries. India and the Philippines are generally offered as examples of countries driven to the edge of ruin by freedom and the right to vote. As I have remarked elsewhere, India's decline from being on the top rung of the less developed countries in the 1950s to an also-ran until the early 1990s was mainly due to its leaders' touching faith in Fabian socialism—kinder and gentler in its political manifestation than communism but equally emphatic that the state had a duty to position itself on the "commanding heights" of the economy by creating and managing a hefty public section.[20] An overreliance on state investment in the economy almost did India in, not liberty or the right to vote. The Philippines, of course, was a "booty capitalist" state under Marcos, neither free nor democratic. Of late, its dalliance with democracy *and* a free market has seen the Philippine economy soar. Citing present-day Korea and Taiwan as illustrations of how much damage democracy can do to a previously stable polity is no more than a red herring. The transgressions of the ruling class or party are exposed in a free society but brushed under the carpet in countries where the people have surrendered their rights to the state. The revelations of various forms of skulduggery arising from an excessive family loyalty that are likely to emerge if Indonesia becomes a democracy are not a sign of weakness but a sign of maturity in society. However, one can empathize with leaders who are worried about the effects of democracy, not on their societies—though the adjustment to freedom and the sharing of responsibility with groups other than one's family will be a tricky one—but on *themselves* and their near and dear. Even countries in which a certain minimum level of freedom of expression and the right to elect one's representatives are guaranteed—notwithstanding the less-than-perfect methods of their implementations—there are clear signs that family loyalties loom large in the minds of the citizenry. The countries of the Indian subcontinent, in certain respects, present us with a stark contrast to most of their close and distant neighbors to the east. Pakistan, India, Bangladesh and Sri Lanka are functioning democracies, perhaps, because the political model they chose was that of Britain, of which they once were colonies. Apart from recent entrants to the democratic club like Korea, Taiwan and the Philippines, the South Asian countries have been democracies for much of the 50-plus years since their independence. However, a curious phenomenon has occurred repeatedly in these family-driven societies. Though intermediate institutions like the judiciary, the media and other nongovernmental bodies exist, these societies have been unable to break away from their family ties in one significant way—leadership. There appears to be a preference for dynastic succession among the electorate. The Bhuttos in Pakistan, the Gandhi/Nehrus in India, the Rahmans and Haqs in Bangladesh and the Bandaranaikes in Sri Lanka seem to exercise an almost feudal hold on the electorate's collective minds. The spectacle of senior leaders of India's once powerful Congress Party traipsing over to pay their respects to Rajiv Gandhi's Italian-born widow, Sonia, is stunning and colonial. But it's all par for the course even in the less statist, more communitarian parts of Asia.

Asian societies face real challenges and threats to the continuance of the headlong growth many of them have experienced over the past few decades. "Asian values," far from being pillars of support, could prove to be quicksand capable of consuming them. The threats are threefold. The triple dangers are crime, corruption and (a lack of) communitarianism. No amount of bluster about so-called Asian values can silence the enemy within.

NOTES

1. In elaborating upon Gerschenkron's thesis (Alexander Gerschenkron, *Economic Backwardness in Historical Perspective* [New York: Praeger, 1962], pp. 7, 8) that growth can be condensed by "followers" on the road to economic development, Cho Soon, *The Dynamics of Korean Development* (Washington, D.C.: Institute for International Economics, 1994), pp. 5, 6, observes that capital and technology can be imported, products can be exported, production methods are being constantly improved and imperial powers do not control the shipping lines as they used to.

2. Increased consumption, especially among younger Chinese, has kept the economy rattling along at a fair clip (around 9–10%) but seems to have caused ripples of concern among economists and officials (*The Wall Street Journal*, July 15, 1996). Coupled with declining investment in the private sector and softening demand (*The Asian Wall Street Journal*, June 23, 1997), this has led to a downward revision of GDP growth to 9% for 1997 and 8.7% for 1998.

3. The divergent accounting techniques result in life insurance, Social Security, house renovation and so on being classified differently from country to country. Kenichi Ohmae (*The End of the Nation State* [New York: Free Press, 1995], pp. 18, 19) adduces persuasive evidence in support of his assertion that the apparent chasm in savings rates is not as wide as one might imagine.

4. M. H. Abrams (gen. ed.), *Norton Anthology* (New York: Norton, 1993), p. 856.

5. Nirad Chaudhuri, *The Continent of Circe* (Delhi: Jaico, 1966) and Bo Yang, *The Ugly Chinaman* (St. Leonards, Australia: Allen and Unwin, 1992) have been caustic critics of the Indian and Chinese peoples' traits—work ethics, social skills, etc. Chaudhuri makes the point that Indian culture has degenerated into a blind imitation of the West while claiming to be self-sufficient, while Bo Yang suggests that China needs to learn rational behavior and courtesy to outsiders from the West. Both adopt an extreme position, perhaps, with a view to shock their respective audiences into listening and acting, but the thrust of their remarks strikes home— there is a hidden side to Asian cultures that may yet prove to be these nations' Achilles' heel.

6. *The Economist*, March 29, 1997.

7. The "meme" is the cultural analogue of the gene and is transferred from one individual to another. Beliefs, fashions and tastes are considered memes, which, like genes, are self-replicating (Richard Dawkins, *The Selfish Gene* [New York: Oxford University Press, 1976]).

8. In contrast to the Confucian belief that we are born into a web of social relationships in which duties are prescribed, the Lockean system asserts that we are born with rights. Francis Fukuyama (*Trust* [London: Penguin, 1995]) places the Western emphasis on rights in stark contrast to Confucianism's duty orientation. The government becomes parent in the latter and is based on the consent of the people in the former (pp. 284, 285).

9. One of the factors most instrumental in the rise of all forms of crime in China (increasing, reportedly, at a rate of 20 to 40% per year) is the creation of a huge transient population. Drug trafficking and prostitution are widespread. Income disparity has risen in recent years (urban incomes increased by 6–10% annually, while other households actually experienced a drop in income), exacerbating the problems occasioned by the floating population (James Miles, *The Legacy of Tiananmen: China in Disarray* [Ann Arbor: University of Michigan Press, 1996]).

10. Violent crime in Taiwan tripled in the period 1992–97, fostering a widespread belief that social order had broken down. The government, visibly responsible for economic growth, is being blamed for the social problems (*The Asian Wall Street Journal*, May 12, 1997).

11. For a vivid account of the repressive and corrosive nature of the "Suharto miracle," see William Greider, *One World, Ready or Not* (New York: Simon and Schuster, 1997), pp. 388–97.

12. The powerlessness of—or the willing abdication of power by—governments vis-à-vis global firms is described in graphic detail in Greider's account of the fire that claimed in excess of 200 lives in May 1993 (ibid., pp. 337–43).

13. John Naisbitt's *Megatrends Asia* (New York: Simon and Schuster, 1996) is a wealth of factual information and data. Even when confronted by gloomy data such as the foregoing, however, Naisbitt remains upbeat since the economic picture appears to be generally rosy. But the clouds on the horizon could be harbingers of trouble, if not doom, as the present work warns.

14. Fukuyama, *Trust*, pp. 173–74.

15. The personalistic, even nepotistic nature of family-centered societies is underscored by Fukuyama. The influence of Japan on Korea does not extend to the role played by the Korean family. Korea appears to be more Confucian in this than Japan and perhaps, according to Fukuyama, even China itself. The impact of Chinese and Korean familism on the CFB and the *chaebol*, respectively, has been noted earlier. In Japan, on the other hand, citizenship and loyalty to one's organization often take precedence over one's family (ibid., pp. 83–95, 127–40, 171–80).

16. Class differences exacerbate the power disparity in organizations occasioned by control by a coterie. Labor unrest is a natural outcome, particularly in a society such as South Korea in which communitarianism has never been a unifying force (ibid., pp. 133–36).

17. Ibid., pp. 49–57.

18. Fukuyama notes that the term "amoral familism," coined to illustrate the dysfunctionality of societies in which the family alone matters, could be applied to Chinese societies. Common property is no one's responsibility, and resources are to be used for the benefit of one's family, even if society suffers as a consequence (ibid., pp. 87–88).

19. Familism combined with the need to develop rapidly and the desire not to be seen acquiescing to "Western" concerns over pollution is a potent brew. The

damage already done to the environment in Asia is tremendous. It could turn out to be catastrophic if communitarian voices of sanity are not raised and paid attention to in these familistic nations. See, for instance, Paul Kennedy, *Preparing for the Twenty-first Century* (London: HarperCollins, 1993), pp. 190–92.

20. Jim Rohwer, in *Asia Rising* (New York: Touchstone, 1995), pp. 177–80, outlines the problem of political freedom coupled with economic servitude that bedeviled India for over four decades. A recent *Wall Street Journal* article (October 4, 1996) illustrates what enlightened leadership has accomplished in a still-democratic Philippines.

7

Setting One's House in Order

An admonition commonly used in the conduct of our daily lives and frequently extended to decision making in firms, is that "if it ain't broke, don't fix it." Though its origins clearly lie in the specific context of machinery, the maxim has almost become a guide to action (or perhaps inaction), based on the belief that meddling with success, with a winning formula, can only detract from the high level of performance already achieved. The advantages of not tinkering with a machine in perfect running order were obvious to anyone responsible for production, and no one dared question the rationale behind letting the equipment run until the first signs of trouble. That was until the notion of preventive maintenance was developed and became part of the accepted wisdom on the factory floor. Running a machine into the ground could result in damage and lost production far in excess of the costs incurred in shutting the machine down while it was still functioning properly. Even waiting for the first signs of trouble could mean dealing with the uncertainties of failure diagnosis. The health care industry is also aware of the dangers inherent to reimbursing remedial treatment to the exclusion of preventive examinations and testing. Most health maintenance organizations (HMOs) and insurers cover the cost of routine physicals, while specific examinations and tests are standard for people in high-risk categories (based on age, gender, lifestyle and so on). However, when it comes to organizations, there often seems to be a predilection to wait until it "breaks," that is, until things start going wrong. Perhaps it has something to do with a resistance to changing a strategy that has worked well, a collective, mutually reinforced feeling that things will turn themselves around or an insensitivity to a shifting external environment. Factors of this sort have obviously been at work in the past and continue to bedevil firms today. The counterplatitude "If it ain't broke, it probably will!" has many adherents but not quite so many practitioners. Witness IBM's tenacious loyalty to the mainframe business, even after it had successfully broken into the personal computer market at Apple's expense. Or Compaq's discomfiture when its carefully cultivated ability and image as an innovator were whittled away by inexpensive "clones" with similar capabilities and by the likes of Dell and Gateway, which put their superior market competencies to work. Examples of corporate inertia (or Micawberian optimism, whichever you prefer) abound. The integrated steel producers like U.S. Steel did not see the writing on the wall when the Japanese made their early moves and, later, when the minimill industry started mushrooming. The railroads ignored trucking, Sears didn't wake up to Wal-Mart for a while and Adidas turned a blind eye to Nike until it was too late to do anything about it.

Integral to the process of business strategy is the mechanism of control. Determining whether achievements and goals coincided, and if not, why, is as important as the formulation of the appropriate strategy in the first place. Realism and a capacity for self-criticism are essential traits to exercise effective control. Persisting in the belief that if only we (e.g., IBM) had been more responsive to customers in the mainframe business—while refusing steadfastly to admit that our strategy and assumptions regarding PCs were to blame—could take the firm on a painful downward spiral. Hiding the truth from a patient (that a prior diagnosis or course of treatment was in error) could shield the doctor from responsibility temporarily, but it certainly will not remedy the illness. At least as harmful as not confronting the reasons for poor performance is not trying to understand why results matched or exceeded expectations. Rather than indulge in self-congratulation, the first order of business ought to be ascertaining if happenstance or fortuitous conditions facilitate the desired outcomes. If, for instance, market share soars when a leading competitor exits the industry in order to pay more attention to other product lines, taking credit for the resulting windfall, if any, would be an act of self-deception. Or if a particular foreign currency weakens, making raw material imports from that country less expensive, continued cost reductions for the same reason on a similar scale are unlikely to materialize.

Nations, too, need to ask tough questions of themselves and act on the responses—particularly ones in which someone clearly has his or her hand on the tiller. Governments, clearly at the helm where economic—and, in many instances, social, political, technological and managerial—change is involved, have to analyze why they have succeeded so swimmingly. If they assume that simple extrapolation gives them a window on the future, they may—indeed, will—be in for a rude awakening. Discontinuities are likely to occur. The fact is that inputs cannot increase indefinitely and that total factor productivity has not risen at anywhere near the same rate as GDPs have in any Asian country (there is disagreement as to the rate of increase of TFP but little argument that it has been nowhere in the vicinity of the economies' growth rates). In addition to the matter of inputs and TFP, there is, of course, the impossibility of sustaining export-based growth or dangling ever more attractive incentives for firms to keep doing more of the same. Certainly, most countries have tried to climb the ladder of technology-intensity, to alter their strategic emphasis as they move through developmental phases. Japan, South Korea, Taiwan and even Malaysia, Indonesia and Thailand no longer pursue textile or light machinery exports exclusively. However, the thesis of the preceding paragraph still holds. Though Asia has experienced remarkable success in the past, and the nations in the diverse continent have attempted to develop new capabilities and to enhance existing ones, they still have fallen prey to the crime of hubris. They are unwilling to accept criticism and unable to see themselves as others do. Krugman, Young and others[1] who proposed the deficient TFP hypothesis raised the hackles of some Asian leaders who refused to even consider the possibility that their countries' GDPs are not likely to keep growing without limit. Just as corporations often fail or do not wish to properly exercise their control function, nations, caught up in their own narcissism, cannot take more than a pinch of reality at a time. "Bashing" the West has become a popular sport among certain Asian leaders and among scholars wide-eyed with admiration at how many have been rescued from poverty in a few decades.[2] The United States and Europe are in irreversible decline, according to the scenario painted by the pundits, while China, Indonesia and the rest of Asia are on an inexorable rise. The fact that the Japanese economy appears to be limping from recessionary pillar to post and that the American economy appears to be in robust condition makes little difference. The fact that many of the economies of the region, particularly China and Japan, have mammoth trade surpluses made possible by the continuing health of the American economy makes little difference. Much is made of the fact that cutting-edge technologies are increasingly in evidence in products made and in the daily lives of people in the developing countries of Asia. That much of the technology has been transferred by MNEs—often as a quid pro quo for market access—and is often not fully absorbed is generally not emphasized. Anything that does not fit the scenario of Asian ascendancy is ignored or treated as temporary aberration.

Take Thailand's flirtation—it could well turn out to be a more serious involvement—with trouble in early 1997.[3] Speculation in real estate, unsecured lending and an overvalued stock market led to a stock market and currency crisis. Banks have not been the only institutions affected. Industrial output is down. The automobile industry, hailed not long ago as Asia's largest after Japan, has experienced cutbacks and layoffs. The crisis has caused ripples of consternation to spread to other Asian capitals, particularly fellow ASEAN members, which have taken immediate steps to shore up their currency and to curb, to the extent possible, speculation in their financial territories. Given the transitory nature of finance today, a feature that most Asian countries have relished and exploited, it will be as difficult to control exit decisions as it was enjoyable to welcome the investors in the first place.

If anyone questions the depth of modern Asia's dependence on foreign ideas and expertise, a look at recent Malaysia's efforts to build a future to match its recent past provides stronger evidence. The country's prime minister unfolded long-range plans to shore up its technological future by establishing a multimedia supercorridor near the capital.[4] The purpose is to incubate the emerging and yet-to-be-conceived technologies, be they in information system, telecommunications, biotechnology or composite materials. How is this vision to be transformed into reality in what was, until recently, the backwoods of Asia, in a country whose leader decries Western culture and society whenever an opportunity presents itself? Why, in the centers of world technology, of course, in Amsterdam, Manchester, Zurich, San Jose and Munich, where the pathbreaking ideas that will change our world and our lives in the years to come are being shaped today. Trapped in the middle between the soaring high-tech innovations of the likes of Phillips, Sony, Intel and Motorola, on one hand, and low-cost exporters like China, India and the Philippines with their seemingly endless sources of inexpensive labor, on the other, Malaysia is desperately searching for ways to borrow from the one to outdo the other.[5] Going it alone has proved to be a frustrating enterprise on par with Sisyphus' labors. The more that countries try to break out of their dependence on technology from advanced nations, the more dependent on them they become. The "walling off" of technology practiced by MNCs—pieces of equipment are fabricated in diverse locations, know-how is transferred, leaving the know-why to be figured out—does not paint a complete technological picture in the recipient country. The old adage about giving a man a fish to feed him for one day and teaching him how to fish in order to feed him for a lifetime comes to mind here. MNCs, for all their talk about global business as a positive-sum game, are loath to part with their hard-won expertise and, as it were, their raison d'être. In fact, it would not be incongruous to extend the saw to the effect that the person who has learned to fish not only can feed himself but might even buy a few boats and establish his own fishing fleet. No MNC wants to create competition for itself, even for a cause as worthy as serving growing, munificent markets. The Japanese have clearly demonstrated their reluctance to share any knowledge that might help spawn new competition. Fragmentation of transferred technology and the withholding of the "software" that explains and helps develop improvements in "hardware" are hallmarks of Japanese MNCs' jealous guardianship of their intellectual property and future competitiveness.[6] The technology that

has flowed into Malaysia over the past three decades is limited and eva-
nescent. Transfer has occurred generally to the extent needed for undertaking production in a low-wage location, which means that emerging
low-cost centers have attracted subsequent investments in (newer) technologies. Countries in the no-man's-land of medium technologies, small markets and rising costs that wish to retain the glories of their "youth" in the
face of intensifying rivalry must draw emerging technologies into their fold
when the bases for nurturing strategic technologies have all but dissipated.
The creation of technological sanctuaries promising a free exchange of
ideas, subsidized facilities and a suspension of the otherwise rigid regulations within the enclave appears to be an alternative to consider, an alternative Malaysia is grasping.

By all accounts, China's social-political-economic experiment centered
around the development of market forces has been a resounding success.
The high inflows of foreign capital, the way in which people have adapted
to employment in private (rather than government-owned) enterprises and
the rate of income growth, particularly in the SEZs, attest to the government's success in encouraging economic growth through the mechanism of
a free market while inducing conformity to societal norms—defined to be
synonymous with governmental norms—by suppressing most other freedoms. Distortions and contradictions are the inevitable outcomes of such
attempts, so to speak, to run with the hares and hunt with the hounds.
Anomalies will appear—and, in fact, have already appeared—at system
interfaces. For instance, at the political-economic interface we observe institutions that have official backing playing prominent roles, even enjoying
monopolistic powers, within the framework of an unguided, unfettered
market. The apparent absence of any restraint on the manufacturing activities of the People's Liberation Army (PLA) is clear evidence that the party's
dependence on the PLA for continuing power gives it the bargaining power
essential to bend market forces to its advantage.[7] Weapons and ammuni-
tion, no doubt the stock-in-trade of militaristic organizations everywhere,
are produced by "subsidiaries" of the PLA, not for use by the Chinese
armed forces but to earn export revenues for the PLA and the government.
The export of Chinese arms, legal and illegal, to the United States is undertaken by a variety of front organizations of the PLA. It serves to kill
two birds neatly with one stone in the perception of Chinese politicians—
weakening American society while raking in export dollars. As services
such as sanitation are privatized, the heavy hand of administrative authority still figures as a prominent influence. The local police and party bigwigs
have a role, often a decisive one, in awarding contracts. In some areas, even
police services are being privatized, opening up even wider avenues for graft
and, what could be worse, an even more arbitrary exercise of power.[8] The
involvement of institutions responsible for defense and for the maintenance
of order in the economic realm as players and not as arbiters makes the

development of stable political and economic institutions more difficult to realize.

Korea's woes, which started in the mid-1980s in the form of a sharp slowdown in growth, have persisted well into the 1990s. Korea was one of the first Asian countries to be caught in an "Asian sandwich." Unable to quite attain Japan's technological prowess and apparently condemned to toil in its powerful neighbor's shadow, Korea has been dogged by other Asian nations hot on its trail, targeting similar labor-intensive industries for export to Western markets. With the *chaebol*'s investments in automobiles, semiconductors and electronic goods seemingly paying handsome dividends, the long-term outlook for the Korean economy brightened considerably at the start of the last decade of this century. However, the country's political troubles have multiplied—caused not by democracy, to reiterate the argument made earlier, but by the arrogance of power that the absence of liberty and accountability occasions—which, compounded by labor and student unrest, has placed a huge question mark over the direction in which Korean society will evolve as this millennium draws to an end, and the next one unfolds. The cauldron of uncertainty boils over when we toss in the recent economic upheaval, which harks back, in large part, to the government's decision, policies and actions aimed at facilitating the rise and continued success of the *chaebol*. The preferential treatment given to the conglomerates was a significant factor in spawning the Korean tiger.[9] Within the context of a strong state such government policies were not construed as favors to business that needed to be reciprocated. (Of course, the selection of the firms to be grown did involve playing favorites, but the government was nowhere near as venal as, say, that of the Philippines in the dispensing of subsidies and incentives.) As the firms prospered, however, the temptation to exact, or not to object to, corporate reciprocation became stronger. The corruption scandals that have rocked Korea in the 1990s are linked to periods when sustained corporate success generated demands, implicit and explicit, for a quid pro quo. As pro-*chaebol* policies gathered momentum, the purpose no longer remained the national interest alone. The intrusion of personal and political goals into the decision criteria of a hitherto relatively incorruptible state has not only sullied the government's reputation in Korea and abroad but also led to a debilitation of the body economic. The approval of large, unsecured loans—typically with political backing or instigation—to *chaebols* under the overarching assumption that the uninterrupted rise of these massive entities would persist indefinitely has come back to haunt the banks and their (un)official patrons. Thailand's wake-up call came in the wake of a speculative frenzy not unusual when the first flush of capitalistic enthusiasm and naïveté blinds lenders and borrowers alike to the dangers of building a financial edifice on quicksand. Korea's financial irresponsibility stems from a perception that the *chaebol* can do no wrong and that the future of the country is tied to the fate of a few gargantuan firms whose influence is felt in every nook and cranny of the economy. Such an assumption of infallibility can only lead to an ever more punitive reckoning when that day dawns, as it must. While the rules and understandings favoring relatives of the founders are being moderated with a more rational performance- and competency-driven system, it is still too early to determine whether this change in managerial decision behavior is a flash in the pan, whether it is confined to one or two companies (e.g., Samsung) or whether a radical shift in mind-set is, indeed, about to sweep the land. Suffice it to say that the social stratification of Korean society based on ancestry, exacerbated by the central role of family connections in selection and succession procedures, is not a recent phenomenon, nor is it likely to disappear anytime soon.

The Indonesian government's decision to make a "national car" should surprise no one.[10] After all, not only has Malaysia's national car, the Proton, proved to be a resounding hit with consumers, but its production has spawned a host of ancillary industries, keeping the nation afloat on a rising technological tide. As much as anything else, the Proton has stimulated a burst of pride in the country's achievement (albeit the car itself was conceived and fleshed out on Japanese drawing boards and first saw the light of day on a shop floor in that country). The Indonesian vehicle also bears the national stamp, no doubt, but not in quite the same way. The car, to be made in collaboration with the Korean *chaebol* Kia, will initially be imported, attracting tariffs far below those levied on equivalent Japanese or European imports. As local production picks up, the taxes and duties to be paid by the local manufacturer are again lower than those to be paid by other carmakers in Indonesia. Of course, Kia's local ally is a firm headed by one of Suharto's offspring—probably the least unexpected part of the whole deal. Naturally, the discriminatory tariffs and tax structure developed for the car (which, incidentally, will be beyond the reach of all but the most affluent) have drawn a storm of protest, particularly from the Japanese, whose manufacturers stand to lose the most. Indonesia, like most of its neighbors, has always talked an excellent game of free trade while playing according to its own rules. However, so blatant a suborning of the regimen of free trade, particularly a member country of the WTO, is an expression of supreme contempt toward the rules of, and its partners in, international trade. Perhaps even more shocking is the rather supine behavior of the Japanese. Though it was a case of the pot's calling the kettle black, we can be sure the quick Japanese climb-down from their lofty moral position was not occasioned by a fear of being branded hypocrites. More likely, concern over the future of their other investments and the possibility of losing a low-wage location and growing market guided their decision to follow their loud protests with a deafening silence. The Japanese are no worse than the Europeans or the Americans, who appear to be vying with one another in kowtowing to the Chinese for every contractual scrap thrown their way. However, being hoist with their own petard is especially galling to the likes of Mitsubishi and Nissan.

We have in an earlier chapter investigated the thesis that the nation-state will come to a timely—or, in the view of sentimental traditionalists, untimely—end as the forces of globalization and the ideology of globalism take permanent hold. However, as we have seen, governments jealously guard their national identities. The national car is but one incarnation of the spirit of nationalism. Strategic technology and trade theory loom large over every governmental action. It must be conceded, notwithstanding all the diverse modes of state intervention, that most countries in Asia have demonstrated a willingness to serve foreign markets and open up to ideas from abroad in order to expand their economies and narrow the gap between them and the advanced countries. Even if it meant swallowing a dollop of national pride, Korea, Thailand, Indonesia and many other countries in the region were eager to use the West's own methods (and its customers) to pull themselves up from poverty. India, for much of its postindependence history, resisted this pragmatic route. Trapped in its own socialistic theorizing until 1991, India even today wallows in its own quagmire of autarkism. Though market reforms were initiated in 1991, the governing coalition appears to be halfhearted about foreign investment and about privatizing the creaking, bloated public sector.[11] The far Right believes in self-reliance, which means excluding MNCs in all but the most technology-intensive industries, while the far Left, though not averse to foreign direct investment, would continue to deny firms the right to exit an industry when they deem it necessary. The inherent faith that most Indians repose in their country's abilities to prosper economically flies in the face of India's performance over the last half century and how far the country has fallen behind nearly every other in Asia, barring perhaps Myanmar. India's hollow nationalism is illustrated in the conflict generated within the government over the proposed joint venture between Singapore Airlines and Tata (an Indian equivalent of one of the larger *chaebol*) to establish a domestic airline.[12] Opponents of the proposed alliance contend that it would spell the demise of the government-owned airline, which is at present a virtual monopoly. The distrust of foreign companies and the lurking suspicion that by allowing MNCs to compete in a vital sector of the economy, the way is being cleared to hand the country over to a foreign power, are alive and well in the country. The need to improve airline transportation, curb the incessant fare increases and better serve the passenger apparently takes second place to the need for local, if inefficient and wasteful, ownership.

For a region and, indeed, a continent whose future is predicted to be as bright as its recent past, Asia appears to be curiously riddled with numerous flaws and fault lines, each with the potential to cause the engines of growth to stall. The need to build capabilities in technology development, to conduct original research in science, to be able to manage organizations and to create societal institutions capable of supporting a modern economic civilization has been noted earlier and analyzed in some detail. The thesis of this book has been that Asia's meteoric growth must sputter and slow down not just because this is inevitable—even the most optimistic Asia watchers concede that a deceleration is likely—but because some or all of the drivers of continued expansion are missing (or in short supply) in all the countries examined. The purpose has not been to denigrate Asian achievements. That would be both unrealistic and ungracious. Rather, the intent has been to assess, with a dose of cold reason, the path ahead. If the path appears to be more treacherous, it is not merely because, à la Krugman, Young et al., input, not TFP increases, has had more to do with the brilliance of Asia's rising star. The immediate need among the Asian countries that have scaled the foothills and can see the peaks ahead (Malaysia, Indonesia and perhaps even Korea) is to realize that what got them this far will not see them through the next decade with any degree of success. Humility and a clear vision of their technological and managerial limitations they have to overcome are likely to yield better results than a blind belief in their superior competence and enduring culture. The societal changes likely to occur as technological change and consumerism take hold have yet to play themselves out in much of Asia. The transformations in society wrought by the widespread use of automobiles, the increasing dependence on microcomputers and the pervasive influence of television are aspects of modern technology whose full impact has not yet been felt. On the production side, the alienation and powerlessness experienced by labor, which is controlled by, not in control of, operational processes, have not yet caused the degree of antagonism they are capable of. The fact that labor has been grateful for the income it has earned, coupled with the muzzle clamped on it in countries like Malaysia and Indonesia, has kept the lid on labor unrest thus far. The lid, however, can blow, especially if regimes become weak or unstable or economic growth falters—as it most likely will.

The problems that ail a few select Asian countries cited earlier in this chapter are representative of the maladies besetting Asia and are symptomatic of a rudderless ship. That is, there is no overarching philosophy illuminating the path of Asian capitalism. If there is any belief system that informs the economies of the diverse nations in Asia, it is materialism. Self-interest and the desire to get ahead are prominent features of capitalism with an Asian face. Greed, as Deng Xiaoping put it during his famous post-Tiananmen tour of southern China, is good.[13] The pursuit of wealth has become an all-consuming passion in Beijing, Bombay, Jakarta, Manila, Taipei, Seoul, Kuala Lumpur, Bangkok and all points in between. An obsession with the accumulation of money is not a crime, of course, and Asians are no different from Europeans and Americans in their desire to earn and possess more. What is different is that Western capitalism grew under the protective umbrella of liberal democracy and a work ethic driven by the urge to gain spiritual salvation through increased efforts to succeed in this life. The self-correcting capabilities of democracy—it may take long and it may not lead to results everyone likes—are often maddening even to its proponents and are frequently the object of disdain among its many critics. The purported otherworldliness of the Protestant ethic serves to elevate the desire for wealth to a higher plane than that of plain, unvarnished greed. Though the Christian ethic might well have been no more than a convenient reason for accumulating riches, acting in concert with scientific inquiry, technological prowess and a liberal democratic policy, it provided the conceptual, intangible foundation for Western capitalism. Until Asian countries can develop their own philosophical and ideological bases for capitalism, until they can rise above sheer materialistic and familistic preoccupations, they will be condemned forever to toil in the long, ubiquitous shadows of their European and American mentors.

NOTES

1. See Chapter 1, for example; Paul Krugman's "The Myth of Asia's Miracle," *Foreign Affairs* 73, No. 6 (November–December 1994) and Alwyn Young's "The Tyranny of Numbers: Confronting the Statistical Realities of the East Asian Growth Experience," *The Quarterly Journal of Economics* 110, No. 3 (1995): 641–80.

2. The works I include in this category are books like John Naisbitt's *Megatrends Asia* (New York: Simon and Schuster, 1996), James Abegglen's *Sea Change* (New York: Free Press, 1994) and William Overholt, *The Rise of China* (New York: W. W. Norton, 1993). The list of laudatory (and perhaps reverential) books devoted to the achievements of Asian nations, individually and collectively, is, of course, too long to cite. The point is that most of them take the World Bank's lead (*The East Asian Miracle* [New York: Oxford University Press, 1993]) in gushing over the wonders of modern Asia with, at most, a footnote or two devoted to the negative accoutrements, present and future, of success.

3. See, for instance, the *Wall Street Journal*, May 30, 1997. The Philippines and Malaysia have taken action to prevent a similar crisis from spreading to their shores, but with bank loans often going to speculators—with governmental backing—it is going to be difficult to avoid risky investments from going bust.

4. The intent is to create another Silicon Valley to serve as the technology hub for a vibrant Asia. As an article in the *Wall Street Journal* (June 10, 1997) points out, Malaysia's "look east policy" involves looking even farther east—to California.

5. Ibid.

6. As indicated earlier (in Chapter 4) Japanese firms *do* transfer technology—but in a form that makes imitation difficult. The "black boxes" of technology that Japan hands over to its suppliers and "partners" do not enable them to strike out on their own very capably. See Fumio Kodama, "Emerging Trajectory of the Pacific Rim: Concepts, Evidences, and New Schemes," in Denis Fred Simon (ed.), *The*

Emerging Technological Trajectory of the Pacific Rim (Armonk, N.Y.: M. E. Sharpe, 1994), pp. 41–53.

7. The nature and extent of the People's Liberation Army's tentacles in China and elsewhere, particularly in the United States, are documented extensively in Richard Bernstein and Ross Munro, *The Coming Conflict with China* (New York: Alfred A. Knopf, 1997). Toys and frozen fish are exported to the United States both to earn profits as well as to gain new technologies. The PLA, through various front organizations and through acquired firms, has a significant and sinister presence in the United States.

8. James Miles, *The Legacy of Tiananmen: China in Disarray* (Ann Arbor: University of Michigan Press, 1996). The perils of secretive privatization are writ large on the Chinese reform landscape. The involvement of the police and of the PLA in smuggling and other illegal activities is also described in Nicholas Kristof and Sheryl WuDunn, *China Wakes* (New York: Random House, 1994), pp. 188–201.

9. In spite of a recent commission report that more discipline is needed in lending by banks to the *chaebol*, the government appears to be determined to continue with business as usual. Truly, signs of an addicted state! (*The Asian Wall Street Journal*, July 7, 1997).

10. *Financial Times*, Tuesday, June 10, 1997. Ironically, the Indonesian national car has been named the Timor—the island on which civil rights appear to be abrogated by the Suharto regime. Since the Timor costs about half as much as a comparable foreign car, firms like Ford and GM are upset, the former to the extent of shelving its plans to enter the Indonesian market.

11. "Survey of India,"*The Economist*, February 22, 1997, pp. 23, 24.

12. The flap over Enron was another high-profile effort at asserting national pride, even if it meant risking investment and employment losses. Indian politicians are never hesitant to cut off their own noses to spite their people's faces!

13. As Kristof and WuDunn observe, Deng Xiaoping's remark on his southern tour seemed to rouse the material and acquisitive tendencies of the Chinese people to a fever pitch (*China Wakes*, pp. 340–46). Joel Kotkin, in recounting the triumphs and travails of the various diasporas the world has seen, expresses admiration for the Chinese and Indians living and working abroad. One of the unmistakable messages one receives on a perusal of the book is that the Chinese and Indian diasporas are extremely materially oriented. The famed inscrutability of the Chinese and otherworldliness of the Indian only mask an inherent talent for making money (Joel Kotkin, *Tribes* [New York: Random House, 1992]). Whether or not this aptitude includes the ability to develop new technologies, manage their own organizations and rise above emerging societal challenges without outside help remains to be seen.

Selected Bibliography

Abegglen, James. *Sea Change* (New York: Free Press, 1994).

Adas, Michael. *Machines as the Measure of Men* (Ithaca, N.Y.: Cornell University Press, 1989).

Alic, John, Lewis Branscomb, Harvey Brooks, Ashton Carter and Gerald Epstein. *Beyond Spinoff* (Boston: Harvard Business School Press, 1992).

Barber, Benjamin. *Jihad vs. McWorld* (New York: Ballantine, 1996).

Bernstein, Richard and Ross Munro. *The Coming Conflict with China* (New York: Alfred A. Knopf, 1997).

Boorstin, Daniel. *The Discoverers* (New York: Random House, 1983).

Brown, David and Robin Porter (eds.). *Management Issues in China* (London: Routledge, 1996).

Callon, Scott. *Divided Sun* (Stanford, Calif.: Stanford University Press, 1995).

Chaudhuri, Nirad. *The Continent of Circe* (Delhi: Jaico, 1966).

Chen, Min. *Asian Management Systems* (London: Routledge, 1995).

Dawkins, Richard. *The Selfish Gene* (New York: Oxford University Press, 1976).

Dobbs-Higginson, Michael. *Asia Pacific: Its Role in the Coming World Disorder* (London: Mandarin, 1994).

Ehrlich, Susan and Andrall Pearson. *Honda Motor Company and Honda of America* (Boston: Harvard Business School Press, 1989).

Fallows, James. *Looking at the Sun* (New York: Pantheon, 1994).

Fukuyama, Francis. *Trust* (London: Penguin, 1995).

Gerlack, Michael. *Alliance Capitalism: The Social Organization of Japanese Business* (Berkeley: University of California Press, 1992).

Gerschenkron, Alexander. *Economic Backwardness in Historical Perspective* (New York: Praeger, 1962).

Grass, Daniel. *Greatest Business Studies of All Time* (New York: John Wiley, 1996).

Greider, William. *One World, Ready or Not* (New York: Simon and Schuster, 1997).

Hart, Jeffrey. *Rival Capitalists* (Ithaca, N.Y.: Cornell University Press, 1992).

Heilbroner, Robert. *The Nature and Logic of Capitalism* (New York: W. W. Norton, 1985).

Hughes, Jonathan. *The Vital Few* (New York: Oxford University Press, 1986).

Imai, Masaaki. *Kaizen* (New York: McGraw-Hill, 1986).

Ishikura, Yoko and Michael Porter. *Canon Inc.: Worldwide Copier Strategy* (Boston: Harvard Business School Press, 1983).

Kennedy, Paul. *The Rise and Fall of the Great Powers* (New York: Vintage, 1987).

———. *Preparing for the Twenty-first Century* (London: HarperCollins, 1993).

Kotkin, Joel. *Tribes* (New York: Random House, 1992).

Kristof, Nicholas and Sheryl WuDunn. *China Wakes* (New York: Random House, 1994).

Krugman, Paul. "The Myth of Asia's Miracle." *Foreign Affairs* 73, No. 6 (November–December 1994).

Livesay, Harold. *American Made* (Boston: Little, Brown, 1979).

Macintyre, Andrew (ed.). *Business and Government in Industrializing Asia* (Ithaca, N.Y.: Cornell University Press, 1994).

McCord, William. *The Dawn of the Pacific Century* (New Brunswick, N.J.: Transaction, 1993).

McInerney, Francis and Sean White. *Beating Japan* (New York: Truman Talley, 1993).

McPhee, John. *The Control of Nature* (New York: Farrar, Straus and Giroux, 1989).

Miles, James. *The Legacy of Tiananmen: China in Disarray* (Ann Arbor: University of Michigan Press, 1996).

Naisbitt, John. *Megatrends Asia* (New York: Simon and Schuster, 1996).

Ohmae, Kenichi. *The Borderless World* (New York: HarperCollins, 1990).

———. *The End of the Nation State* (New York: Free Press, 1995).

Ohno, Taiichi. *Toyota Production System: Beyond Large Scale Production* (Cambridge, Mass.: Productivity Press, 1988).

Okimoto, Daniel. *Between MITI and the Market* (Stanford, Calif.: Stanford University Press, 1989).

Overholt, William. *The Rise of China* (New York: W. W. Norton, 1993).

Popper, Karl. *The Logic of Scientific Discovery* (New York: Basic Books, 1989).

Prestowitz, Clyde. *Trading Places* (New York: Basic Books, 1988).

Reischauer, Edwin. *The Japanese* (Cambridge: Belknap Press of Harvard University Press, 1977).

Rohwer, Jim. *Asia Rising* (New York: Touchstone, 1995).

Rushdie, Salman. *The Moor's Last Sigh* (New York: Pantheon, 1995).

Schonberger, Richard. *Building a Chain of Customers* (New York: Free Press, 1990).

Segal, Gerald. *The Fate of Hong Kong* (New York: St. Martin's Press, 1993).

Shetty, Y. K. and Vernon Buehler (eds). *Productivity and Quality through People* (Westport, Conn.: Quorum Books, 1985).

Shingo, Shigeoi. *Zero Quality Control: Source Inspection and the Poka-Yoke System* (Cambridge, Mass.: Productivity Press, 1986).

Simon, Denis Fred (ed.). *The Emerging Technological Trajectory of the Pacific Rim* (Armonk, N.Y.: M. E. Sharpe, 1994).

Smith, Hedrick. *Rethinking America* (New York: Random House, 1995).

Soon, Cho. *The Dynamics of Korean Economic Development* (Washington, D.C.: Institute for International Economics, 1994).

Suzaki, Kiyoshi. *The New Manufacturing Challenge* (New York: Free Press, 1987).

Taylor, C. W. (ed.). *The Third University of Utah Research Conference on the Identification of Scientific Talent* (Salt Lake City: University of Utah Press, 1959).

Thant, Myo, Min Tang, and Hiroshi Kahazin (eds.). *Growth Triangles in Asia* (Hong Kong: Oxford University Press, 1994).

Thurow, Lester. *The Future of Capitalism* (New York: Penguin, 1996).

Tilton, Mark. *Restrained Trade* (Ithaca, N.Y.: Cornell University Press, 1996).

Virmani, B. R. and Sunil Guptan. *Indian Management* (New Delhi: Vision, 1991).

Walton, Mary. *Deming Management at Work* (New York: G. P. Putnam & Sons, 1980).

Waterman, Robert. *What America Does Right* (New York: Plume, 1994).

World Bank. *The East Asian Miracle* (New York: Oxford University Press, 1993).

Yang, Bo. *The Ugly Chinaman* (St. Leonards, Australia: Allen and Unwin, 1992).

Yoshimura, Noboru and Philip Anderson. *Inside the Kaisha: Demystifying Japanese Business Behavior* (Boston: Harvard Business School Press, 1997).

Index

About the Author

BERNARD AROGYASWAMY teaches business strategy, quality management, and international management at LeMoyne College in Syracuse, New York. Consultant to various businesses, particularly those with international operations, he has extensive industrial experience in India and has traveled widely in Asia. He has published in academic journals and given numerous presentations at conferences, seminars, and other meetings. Among his publications is *Value-Directed Management: Organizations, Customers, and Quality* (Quorum, 1993), coauthored with Ronald P. Simmons.